A Twentieth Century Fund Paper

HOMELESSNESS IN THE 1980s

BY

PETER ROSSI

 Priority Press Publications/New York/1989

Library of Congress Cataloging-in-Publication Data
Rossi, Peter Henry, 1921–
  Without shelter: homelessness in the 1980s.

  "A Twentieth Century Fund paper"
  Includes index.
  1. Homelessness—United States. 2. Homelessness—Government policy—United States. I. Title
HV4505.R67   1989   362.5'0973   88-31811
ISBN 0-87078-235-5
ISBN 0-87078-234-7 (pbk.)

Copyright © 1989 by the Twentieth Century Fund, Inc.
Manufactured in the United States of America.

WITHOUT SHELTER

Foreword

No social problem tugs on the heartstrings of the American public more than that of the homeless. Their vulnerability—their lack of shelter, one of the most basic human needs—suggests a fundamental failing on the nation's part. On both sides of the aisle there is a clamor that something be done, and done swiftly, to ameliorate the situation of the homeless, to provide them with a "home," something considered every American's due.

But in order to succeed, policymakers need to know more about who the nearly three million homeless are. Are they simply those who have been crowded out of a shrinking housing market? Or are the homeless those whose personal problems—mental illness, substance abuse—have made it impossible for them to find and retain shelter? There is little agreement on this question, in part because of the political ramifications of the answers. If it is simply the lack of housing that is the problem, then the federal government must accept a sizable portion of the blame.

In the following pages, Peter Rossi, professor of sociology at the University of Massachusetts, provides policymakers with critical information on the "new homeless." Unlike the homeless of the past, who were almost all unattached men, they include a large contingent of women, many with their children. While the old homeless played a role in the labor market—furnishing labor for seasonal activities or for short-term, low-skilled jobs—the new homeless find little demand for their services. They are unskilled and, perhaps more importantly, often disabled, a substantial majority having at least one and sometimes many disabilities: chronic physical health problems, mental health problems, or substance-abuse problems.

v

After limning a portrait of the homeless, Rossi takes up the issue of what is to be done. His recommendations are both practical—distinguishing between the episodically and chronically homeless—and far-reaching—suggesting that AFDC payments be extended to families who subsidize their destitute, unattached adult members. I have little doubt that his recommendations will contribute to fresh thinking on this critical issue; we are grateful to him for his efforts.

Marcia Bystryn, ACTING DIRECTOR
The Twentieth Century Fund
January 1989

Contents

Foreword by Marcia Bystryn | *v*

Prologue | 1

1. Introduction | 3

2. Homelessness in Historical Perspective | 5

3. The New Homelessness of the 1980s | 13

4. Structural Factors in the Rise of the New Homeless | 31

5. Limits of Private, Temporary Support Systems | 37

6. What Can Be Done? | 45

7. Conclusions | 61

Notes | 65

Index | 77

Prologue

It was 2 a.m. on a bitter February night in 1986. Eleven men and a woman sat in dirt-encrusted clothes, scattered about the steps inside Chicago's main bus station. A few feet away, a guard barred anyone without a bus ticket from the waiting room lobby. The group was there to evade the night's cold and find safety and rest. By contrast, days were spent alone and on the move, walking from food kitchens to wherever one could stand or sit without being hassled—a library, a train station, a park bench.

Like the others, Frank Claro, twenty-three, looked a decade older than his years. He'd arrived a few months earlier from Cairo, Illinois, seeking work. A former wallboard installer, Claro said he'd been unemployed since the contracting business where he'd worked closed down a year earlier. Until the money ran out, he'd stayed in a cheap Chicago hotel, then in shelters for the homeless until he was beaten and robbed in one. He expected to find work soon or return to Cairo. He'd never been married.

Martin Lewis, thirty-six, had last worked a few weeks back as a day laborer for a truck farmer. He'd worked at unskilled jobs before becoming unemployed a decade earlier. His children, aged ten and twelve, and former wife lived in Chicago, but he didn't know where, he said. He rarely slept in shelters because they barred alcoholics.

Mary Slovic, one of the only whites in the group, had been in and out of psychiatric hospitals until two years earlier. She avoided her parents' home and shelters, she said, because she feared being recommitted. Never married, Slovic, who was forty-two, had a teenaged daughter who lived in a foster home. Her conversation moved in and out of reality.

Alex Sanders was to die two weeks later at the age of thirty-six, after suffering a brain seizure and falling in the path of an automobile. Until

1

a decade before, he'd lived with his wife and two children, and worked in the South Chicago steel mills. But after his weekend drinking binges got longer and longer, he said, his wife kicked him out. He'd been through detoxification programs a half-dozen times. When he worked as a temporary construction laborer, he saved the money for a night in a cheap hotel—and another binge.

• 1 •
Introduction

Homelessness has been getting a lot of attention since the early 1980s—in the mass media, among social scientists, and in government.

Stories about homelessness now appear regularly on the television news and in newspapers and magazines. While no articles on homelessness were listed in the Reader's Guide to Periodical Literature as recently as 1975, forty-eight were listed under that heading in 1986. Television documentaries and national fund-raising events such as "Comic Relief" also have focused on the issue. Indeed, UNESCO declared 1987 the International Year for the Homeless, a reminder that the problem is by no means confined to the United States.

Homelessness is not a new topic for social scientists, some of whom were studying the problem well before the Great Depression; for example, Nels Anderson's classic, *The Hobo,* was published in 1923. Still, there has been an outpouring of recent research on the homeless, supported by private foundations and government agencies.[1] As of early 1988, some forty reasonably well conducted studies had appeared, all based on actual research on homeless populations—usually in a specific city—and all with data collected after 1980. There are hundreds of other studies too small in scope or otherwise too restricted to provide more than anecdotal material.

Members of Congress during the 1987–88 session introduced at least thirty-two separate bills addressing some aspect of the problem. These bills would disperse federal responsibility for the homeless over a wide range of agencies, with separate programs for homeless veterans, homeless alcohol abusers, homeless families with children, and so on. Other efforts to cope with the problem have been focused at the state and local levels, in the public and private sectors.

Given the widespread concern, this paper examines the issue of homelessness in the United States, with a view toward both reducing the size of the homeless population and improving conditions for those remaining homeless. For these purposes, persons are classified as homeless if they are living outside conventional dwellings, either spending nights in shelters for homeless persons or in locations that are not intended for dwelling—on the streets, in abandoned houses, or in public places such as bus stations or hospital waiting rooms.

• 2 •

Homelessness in Historical Perspective

A Lack of Empathy for America's Homeless

America, like other nations, has long had a sizable complement of homeless persons, even though the importance of having a home has been inextricably bound to our ideas of a minimally decent existence.[1] The *Oxford Unabridged Dictionary* devotes three pages to definitions of the word *home* and its derivatives. Almost all the definitions stress one or more of the themes of safety, family, love, shelter, comfort, rest, sleep, warmth, affection, food, and sociability.

In a different vein, Robert Frost provided a marvelous definition of home in his 1914 poem, "The Death of the Hired Man": "Home is the place where,/when you have to go there,/ they have to take you in." To most people, not having a place where they have to take you in would be very close to the bottom of existence, the worst thing imaginable. Sympathy for those so afflicted comes easily to all but the coldest of heart.

Nevertheless, throughout most of American history, the homeless have received little sympathy, being regarded instead with disdain, contempt, fear, hostility, and loathing. In colonial days, homeless and destitute people were often "warned out" of town—shunted from community to community, not allowed to settle anywhere for fear their numbers would overburden the town relief rolls.[2]

That preoccupation with rights of settlement and the welfare benefits accompanying those rights has persisted throughout most of our history. As a result, large proportions of the indigent and needy became migrants in a kind of geopolitical limbo where no jurisdiction would take responsibility for their care. (The *settlement* issue in welfare was ended only two decades ago by a 1966 Supreme Court decision that struck down most state and local residency restrictions on eligibility for welfare benefits.)[3]

There was no more sympathy for the homeless in the nineteenth century than there had been in the colonial era. The end of the Civil War brought a considerable increase in homelessness and transiency. Restless discharged war veterans, male immigrant laborers, and other persons migrating to seek work were characterized as tramps, hoboes, and bums and—again—warned to leave town. Police departments "solved" many crimes by attributing them to the uncontrollable actions of transients. Mark Twain ended his humorous account of how he killed his conscience and was able to give in to his dislike of tramps by advertising to medical schools that he had bodies of several in his basement to sell for use as teaching cadavers.[4]

The prevailing lack of sympathy in the nineteenth century for the plight of homeless and transient persons is all the more puzzling because there was no significant social welfare "safety net" in place to protect individuals or families from the catastrophic consequences of unemployment, illness, or death of the household wage earner. Thus, nearly every nineteenth-century household ran a significant risk of becoming destitute through personal catastrophe, and thereby homeless.[5] Of course, then as now, nineteenth-century Americans made quite strong distinctions between *local homeless*, known families and individuals who fell upon hard times, and the *transient homeless*, persons believed to be homeless out of choice for an irresponsible life-style.

By the late nineteenth century, homelessness was institutionalized and segregated in the newly established Skid Row areas of American cities.[6] These neighborhoods were populated mostly by homeless, unattached, transient laborers who supplied seasonal muscle power for industries such as lumbering, railroad construction, shipping, and highway maintenance—an arrangement frequently brokered by labor contractors. (By *unattached*, I mean people not living with a spouse or partner, or having direct responsibility for children.) The numbers occupying Skid Row increased only until the early decades of the twentieth century; by the late 1920s, technological changes—especially the development of earth-moving and materials-handling equipment—had drastically reduced the demand for casual, unskilled labor. The hobo and the tramp gradually disappeared as important components of the labor supply.

With the advent of the Great Depression in the 1930s, homelessness again increased starkly.[7] As in the present day, there were no definitive counts of the numbers of depression-era homeless, but there are indicators of the magnitudes. In 1933, the Federal Emergency Relief Administration housed 125,000 people in its transient camps; a 1934 survey of social agencies in 765 towns and cities (conducted by the Committee on the Care of Transient and Homeless) estimated that there were 200,000 homeless in all of those places, and other estimates ranged upward of 1.5 million in the worst years of the Great Depression.[8] These numbers are strikingly similar to contemporary estimates of the size of the homeless population, which range from about 350,000 up to several million.[9] Of course the American population in the 1930s was about half its current size, so the prevalence of homelessness then must have been at least at twice the current rates.

Nels Anderson's *Men on the Move* describes the changes the Great Depression brought to the homeless, especially the decline of the transient homeless and the rise of what he thought to be a permanently unemployed class of homeless persons. As described in the social research of the time, the transient homeless consisted mainly of young men (and a small proportion of women) moving from place to place in search of employment. Many left their parental homes because they no longer wanted to be burdens on impoverished households and because they saw no employment opportunities in their depressed hometowns. Others were urged to leave by parents struggling to feed and house their younger siblings. In either event, many returned home when their job searches proved fruitless.

Those who came to the largest urban areas were too numerous to be accommodated in the established Skid Rows. Thus, in the worst years of the depression, many urban transients were housed in emergency shelters, as they are today. In its brief, two-year existence, the Federal Emergency Relief Administration set up numerous camps for transients, usually in rural areas far from the few jobs that were available, and safely out of sight of city dwellers.[10] Police departments often used their jails as overnight shelters. And, of course, many homeless people took care of their own housing problems by building the shanty towns, pictures of which are included in most histories of the Great Depression.

Despite the existence of at least some federal programs, not much sympathy was accorded the homeless in the 1930s, especially not to unattached men and women. The welfare departments of states and local communities often dealt with the homelessness problem by escorting transients to their borders—a solution known today as "Greyhound therapy." Only one category of homeless persons garnered much public sympathy, namely, the farm families in the drought-stricken Dust Bowl states who packed up their meager belongings, loaded their dilapidated cars, drifted westward to California, and became the Okies of whom John Steinbeck wrote so eloquently in *The Grapes of Wrath*. Then as now, apparently, homeless families evoked more compassion than did the more numerous unattached homeless.

Homelessness after World War II

U.S. entry into World War II drastically reduced the homeless population in this country, absorbing them into the armed forces and the burgeoning war industries.[11] The permanently unemployed that so worried Anderson when he wrote in the early 1930s virtually disappeared within months. When the war ended, employment rates remained relatively high, and many returning veterans were eligible for generous benefits under the GI Bill. Thus, homelessness and Skid Row areas shrank to a fraction of the 1930s experience. But neither phenomenon disappeared.

In the first two postwar decades, the Skid Rows remained as a collection of cheap hotels, inexpensive restaurants and bars, casual employment agencies, and religious missions dedicated to the moral redemption of Skid Row residents, who were increasingly an older population. Typically, Skid Row was located close to the railroad freight yards and the trucking terminals that provided casual employment for its inhabitants.

In the 1950s, as urban elites turned to the renovation of the central cities, the question of what to do about the unsightly buildings, low-quality land use, and unkempt people in the Skid Rows sparked a revival of social science research on Skid Row and its denizens. Especially influential were studies of New York City's Bowery by Howard Bahr and Theodore Caplow, of Philadelphia by Leonard Blumberg and his associates, and of Chicago's Skid Row by Donald Bogue.[12] Undertaken between 1958 and 1964, and financed under grants from the Housing and Home Finance Agency, the predecessor to the Department of Housing and Urban Development (HUD), all of these studies had much the same objective—to find out who was on Skid Row and what could be done about them when the area was demolished to make way for urban renewal.

All the studies of the era reported similar findings, with only slight local variations. The title of Bahr and Caplow's monograph—*Old Men Drunk and Sober*—succinctly summarizes much of what was learned, that Skid Row was populated largely by older alcoholic men. Bogue's paper, *Skid Row in American Cities*, provides an especially thorough description and is the source of much of the discussion that follows.

In 1958, Bogue estimated that there were approximately two hundred thousand homeless persons in the Skid Rows of the forty-one largest cities, an estimate based on the Census Bureau's count of unattached persons living outside households in Skid Row areas in those cities. Bogue listed twelve thousand homeless persons in Chicago, almost all of them men. In 1964, Bahr and Caplow estimated that there were about eight thousand homeless men living in New York's Bowery, and possibly thirty thousand additional homeless persons living elsewhere in the city.[13] In 1960, Blumberg and his colleagues found about two thousand homeless persons living in the Skid Row of Philadelphia. Clearly, despite the postwar economic expansion, homelessness persisted. The Skid Rows may well have been dying out; indeed, given the advanced average age of the residual Skid Row population, the impending demise of Skid Row was widely and confidently predicted. But it was obvious that the final death throes would be neither merciful nor swift.

The definition of homelessness used by Bahr and Caplow, Blumberg, Bogue, and other analysts of the era was somewhat different from the current usage. In the studies of the 1950s and early 1960s, homelessness mostly meant living outside family units, whereas today's meaning of the term is more directly tied to the absolute lack of housing or to living in shelters and related temporary quarters. In fact, almost all of the homeless men studied by Bogue in 1958 had stable shelter of some sort. Four out of five rented windowless cubicles in flophouse hotels. The cubicles rented for fifty to ninety cents a night and would hardly qualify as a *home*, at least not by contemporary standards. Most of the cubicle accommodations were partitioned spaces measuring about five by seven feet, capable of holding a cot and little more, lit by a bare twenty-five-watt light bulb. The partitions did not extend to the ceiling or to the floor, and wire mesh was used to fill the gaps, providing security and ventilation.

Most of those not living in the cubicles lived in private rooms in inexpensive single-room-occupancy (SRO) hotels or in the mission dormitories. Bogue reported that only a few homeless men, about a hundred, lived out on the streets, sleeping in doorways, under bridges, and in other "sheltered" places. Blumberg searched the streets, hotels, and boarding houses of Philadelphia's Skid Row area in 1960 and found that most of Philadelphia's two thousand homeless lived in cubicle hotels and mission shelters. Only sixty-four persons were found sleeping in the streets.

Municipal jails also provided shelter of a sort to Skid Row residents, following arrests for public drunkenness, vagrancy, or similar misdemeanors. Before the decriminalization of public drunkenness in 1966, large portions of the nightly arrests in large cities—over 25 percent in New York—were for this and related offenses. Chicago's jails and police stations apparently accommodated several hundred Skid Row residents each evening.[14]

As described by Bogue, the median age of Chicago's homeless in the late 1950s was about fifty years, and more than 90 percent were white. A quarter were Social Security pensioners, making their monthly thirty- to fifty-dollar minimum Social Security payment last through the month by renting the cheapest accommodations possible. Another quarter were chronic alcoholics.[15] The remaining half comprised persons suffering from physical disability (20 percent), chronic mental illness (20 percent), and what Bogue called social maladjustment (10 percent). Empirically, there would have to have been considerable overlap in these categories, but Bogue is silent on the point.

Aside from those who lived on their pension checks, most Skid Row inhabitants earned their living through menial, low-paid employment, much of it intermittent. The mission dormitories and municipal shelters provided food and beds for those out of work or unable to work. In the opinions of Skid Row residents themselves, the mission dormitories were the least desirable among the living alternatives available, since they lacked privacy and safety and usually required attendance at evangelical religious services.

Almost all social scientists who studied the Skid Rows in the postwar period remarked on the social isolation of the homeless. (One of Bahr's books on the homeless is called *Disaffiliated Man*.) Bogue found that virtually all homeless men were unmarried, and a majority had never married. Although many had family, kinship ties were of the most tenuous quality, with few of the homeless maintaining ongoing contacts with their kin. Most had no one they considered their good friends, except, perhaps, other homeless people. Although there may have been some camaraderie among the homeless, the researchers and the homeless themselves both remarked on the superficiality of these ties.

Much the same portrait emerged from the Bahr-Caplow study of the Bowery and from other Skid Row studies throughout the country. The studies painted a picture in the same three pigments: (1) extreme poverty, arising from unemployment or sporadic employment, chronically low earnings, and low benefit levels (such as were characteristic of Social Security pensions at the time); (2) disability, arising from advanced age, alcoholism, and physical or mental illness; and (3) social disaffiliation, and tenuous or absent ties to family and kin, with few or no friends.

Even though the data from these studies showed alcoholism to be a problem for a large proportion, but nonetheless a minority, of the homeless, many wrote as if alcoholism were a well-nigh universal condition of Skid Row. Few researchers were sympathetic to so-called alcoholic bums and derelicts, and the lack of sympathy extended to the other inhabitants of Skid Row. The only Skid Row residents to whom researchers extended sympathy were the impoverished aged pensioners.

Most of the social scientists studying Skid Rows believed that the areas were declining in size and would soon disappear. Bahr and Caplow wrote that the population of the Bowery had dropped from fourteen thousand in 1949 to eight thousand in 1964, a trend that they predicted would end with the disappearance of Skid Row by the mid-1970s. Bogue cited high vacancy rates in the cubicle hotels as evidence that Chicago's Skid Row also was on the decline. In addition, Bogue claimed that the economic function of Skid Row was fast disappearing; with the mechanization of many low-skilled tasks, the casual labor market was shrinking, and with no residual economic function to perform, the Skid Row social system would also disappear.

Evidence through the early 1970s indeed suggested that the forecasted decline was correct, that Skid Row was on the way out. Barrett Lee studied Skid Row areas of forty-one cities and found that the Skid Row populations had declined by 50 percent between 1950 and 1970. Furthermore, in cities where the market for unskilled labor had declined most precipitously, the loss of the Skid Row population was correspondingly larger.[16]

It is important to examine Bogue's recommendations for Chicago's Skid Row. He proposed a plan that would remove the unsightly flophouses and cheap SROs over a five-year period through demolition under urban renewal. The land reclaimed by demolition was to be used to expand the central business district, in order to provide more office buildings and downtown apartments. To house the homeless and those displaced by urban renewal, he suggested that the flophouses and SROs be replaced by scattered subsidized housing for unattached men and that social services be provided for alcoholics and the physically or mentally disabled. The result was to have been a beautified downtown, better housing for the homeless, and better care for the disabled.

By the end of the 1970s, striking changes had taken place in city after city. Indeed, it looked as if Bogue's advice to demolish Chicago's Skid

Row had been followed nearly everywhere. In contrast, his housing and social service recommendations were largely ignored. The flophouse and cubicle hotels had, for the most part, been demolished, to be replaced initially by parking lots and later by office buildings, luxury condominiums, and apartments, a process now known as gentrification. The stock of cheap SRO hotels, where the more prosperous of the old homeless had lived, had also been seriously diminished.[17] Still, Skid Row did not disappear altogether; in most cities, the missions remained and smaller Skid Rows sprouted up in those places in the cities where the remaining SRO hotels and rooming houses still stood.

In the 1960s and 1970s, the need for cheap accommodations for old-age pensioners declined as the coverage of the Social Security system increased to include more of the labor force, and as Congress voted more generous Social Security benefits and pegged those benefits to the cost-of-living index. In addition, subsidized senior citizen housing, the most popular public housing program, began to provide affordable accommodations to the elderly. This increase in the economic well-being of the aged is most dramatically shown in the remarkable decline of the proportion of those age sixty-four and over who are below the poverty line: from 25 percent in 1968 to less than 13 percent in 1985, with the most precipitous decline—nine percentage points—occurring in the three-year period 1970-73.[18]

As a result of these and related changes a large portion of the old Skid Row population disappeared into the general housing stock, or into subsidized housing for the elderly. Higher benefits and subsidized housing made it possible for the aged pensioners to successfully obtain acceptable housing. In addition, more generous benefits were made available to the physically disabled and the chronically mentally ill through expanded Supplemental Security Income (SSI) and Social Security Disability Income (SSDI) programs,[19] also enabling these groups to move up in the housing market.

• 3 •
The New Homelessness
of the 1980s

The "old" homeless of the 1950s, 1960, and 1970s—so ably described by many sociologists—may have blighted some sections of the central cities, but from the perspective of most urbanites, they had the virtue of being concentrated in Skid Row, an urban feature that one could avoid and hence ignore. Most of the old homeless on Skid Row had some shelter, although inadequate by any standards; very few were literally sleeping on the streets. Indeed, in those decades, if any had tried to bed down on the steam vents or in doorways and vestibules of any downtown business area, the police would have quickly trundled them off to jail.

The demise or displacement of Skid Row, however, and the many other trends and developments of the 1960s and 1970s, did not put an end to homelessness in American cities. Quite the contrary: by the end of the 1970s, and certainly by the early 1980s, a new type of homelessness had begun to appear.

The "new" homeless could be seen sleeping in doorways, in cardboard boxes, in abandoned cars, or resting in railroad or bus stations or in other public places, indications of a resurgent homelessness to which hardly anyone could remain oblivious. Some of the homeless also behaved in bizarre ways, muttering, shouting, panhandling, carrying bulky packages, or pushing supermarket carts filled with junk and old clothes. The immediate impression was that there were persons in our society who had no shelter and who therefore lived, literally, in the streets.

The decriminalization of public drunkenness and relaxed enforcement of ordinances concerning other victimless misdemeanors meant that police patrols no longer regularly picked up these people and whisked them from sight. Homelessness was no longer confined to the drunks and derelicts of an avoidable Skid Row. It was, rather, in the very midst of day-to-day urban existence.

Even more striking was the appearance of homeless women in significant numbers. Homelessness among American women is not a new phenomenon, of course; studies by D. L. Jones in Massachusetts and Priscilla Clements in Philadelphia confirm that women have been a sizable fraction of the homeless at least since colonial times, as much as half the total vagrant population in the eighteenth century, the years covered in Jones's study.[1] But the Skid Rows of the 1950s and 1960s were largely male enclaves, and thus homelessness had come to be stereotyped as a male problem. Indifference to the plight of derelicts and bums is one thing. Indifference to the existence and problems of homeless women is quite another.

Soon, entire families began showing up among the homeless, and public attention grew even sharper. Women and their children began to arrive at the doors of public welfare departments asking for aid in finding shelter, arousing immediate sympathy in some quarters. Stories began to appear in the newspapers about families migrating from the Rust Belt cities to cities in the Sun Belt in old cars loaded with their meager belongings, seeking employment, in scenes starkly and distressingly reminiscent of the Okies of the 1930s.

Public Response to the Problem

Popular response to the new homeless grew as evidence of rising homelessness became undeniable. One spur to increased public support was a celebrated 1979 New York case in which public-interest lawyers sued the city, claiming that New York had an obligation to provide shelter to homeless men. The public-interest lawyers' victory led to the doubling of a network of "emergency" municipal shelters in New York over five years to their current capacity of six thousand beds nightly, almost entirely in dormitory quarters. Subsequent court decisions have extended New York City's shelter obligations to include homeless women.[2] Today, overnight shelters for homeless people are fixtures in the social service landscape of every major American city.

The new emergency shelters that have sprung up are certainly better than nothing at all, but not by much. In many respects, the old cubicle hotels were better accommodations. The men's shelters established in New York in the past decade resemble in physical layout the dormitory accommodations provided by missions in the old Skid Rows, accommodations the old homeless regarded as only a last resort. In social organization, these shelters tend to resemble minimum-security prisons except that the gates are open during the day. Indeed, a recent survey of New York shelter clients reported that the shelter residents rated prisons as *superior* in safety, cleanliness, and food quality; the shelters were regarded as clearly superior only in freedom, meaning the right to leave at any time.[3]

Shelter provided for homeless single women is perhaps somewhat better than that supplied to men but, again, is hardly acceptable even on an emergency basis. The single women's shelters resemble most closely the old cubicle flophouses with their cramped but individual and semiprivate accommodations. Accommodations available to women with children, comprising almost all of the homeless families, will be discussed later.

New York City is exceptional in that municipal government has directly provided shelters for the homeless; in most other cities, that task falls to private charities operating on their own or sometimes with government subsidies. Many of the religious missions, for example, the Salvation Army and the Society of Saint Vincent de Paul, have expanded their existing missions and shelters; many other charities and church groups opened shelters for the first time.

In Chicago in 1958, for example, there were four or five mission shelters in the city, providing 975 beds, according to Donald Bogue. In 1985 and 1986, my colleagues and I found forty-five shelters providing a total of two thousand beds primarily for adult homeless persons.[4] In some respects, staying in shelters provided by private charities is preferable to using those provided and operated by municipalities, partly because private shelters can impose restrictions on whom they admit (often excluding persons who are drunk, aggressive, or floridly psychotic or delusional), whereas municipal shelters ordinarily have to admit everyone.

New types of sheltering arrangements have come into being to accommodate the rising number of homeless families. Some shelters now specialize in providing quasi-private quarters for family groups, usually in one or two rooms per family with shared bathrooms and cooking facilities. In many cities, welfare departments have provided temporary housing for family groups by renting rooms in hotels and motels.

In some cities, the use of hotel and motel rooms to shelter homeless families is a widespread and increasing arrangement. For example, in 1986, New York City's welfare department put up an average of thirty-five hundred families in so-called welfare hotels *each month*. That figure compares with a few hundred such families five years earlier.[5] An ironic feature of the use of welfare hotels in this fashion is that the rents paid by the welfare department for the rooms often exceed current rents at the lowest end of the housing market, and by a substantial margin. Indeed, in New York City, rent for a single welfare hotel room is often as much as twelve hundred to eighteen hundred dollars per month.

Funds for the new homeless are being allocated on a scale that would have been inconceivable two decades ago. Private charity has been one generous source. For example, the Robert Wood Johnson Foundation, in association with the Pew Memorial Trust, supports Health-Care-for-the-Homeless (HCH) medical clinics in nineteen large cities, a $25 million venture. The states have provided funds through existing programs and special appropriations. And in summer 1987, Congress passed the Stuart B. McKinney Homeless Assistance Act, appropriating $442 million for the homeless in fiscal 1987 and $616 million in 1988, to be channeled through a great many agencies. The McKinney Act provides some housing assistance, subsidies for existing shelters, and funds for rehabilitation programs including vocational training, medical care, and services for the chronically mentally ill.[6] The McKinney Act adds to existing federal social welfare programs that support homeless persons, such as SSI, SSDI, Aid to Families with Dependent Children (AFDC), Food Stamps, and Medicaid.

Although there is ample evidence that help is needed more now than a decade ago, no one knows for sure how many homeless persons are in the United States today or even in any specific city, let alone the rate of growth in those numbers over the past decade. There are serious obstacles to attaining this knowledge. For example, counts made by the U.S. Census Bureau and others proceed on the assumption that nearly everyone can be reached through a home address, an assumption that is clearly incorrect in the case of the homeless.

Another obstacle is the definition of homelessness: whether the concept should be defined narrowly and thus restricted to those who are without conventional housing (homelessness as houselessness) or defined broadly to include all persons who are inadequately housed, socially marginal, or at high risk for literal homelessness (homelessness as a metaphor for a much larger poverty problem). Depending on whether one adopts a narrow or broad definition, the numbers of homeless will be affected by orders of magnitude.[7]

The many difficulties notwithstanding, several estimates have been made of the size of the nation's homeless population. The National Coalition for the Homeless, an advocacy group, puts the figure somewhere between 1.5 and 3 million. A much-maligned report by HUD, partially based on cumulating the estimates of presumably knowledgeable local experts, and partially on a survey of emergency shelters, put the national figure at somewhere between 250,000 and 300,000.[8] A more recent national estimate by Richard Freeman and Brian Hall tends to support the HUD figures, with an estimate of 350,000 homeless in 1986.[9] Studies reviewed by the General Accounting Office suggest an annual growth rate of the national homeless population of between 10 and 38 percent.[10]

All these estimates are based on the assumption that the number of the homeless living in the streets (very hard to count) is several multiples of the number living in emergency shelters (relatively easy to count), an inadequately researched assumption. Our data from Chicago suggest the two groups are about equal in size, with considerable seasonal fluctuation in the relative proportions.[11]

In the same vein, those estimating "the" size of the homeless population are often marvelously obscure about the precise referent: do they mean how many homeless on a given night; how many homeless in the course of the year; or how many destined to be homeless at least once in their lifetimes? The abundant evidence that the homeless population is not stable but rather "turns over" in short time periods means these are very different questions, but they are often treated as the same question in the literature.[12]

The difficulty in defining the population is partly tied to limitations of language. The very phrase, *the homeless,* implies a certain permanence of condition that the data simply do not support. Researchers from the University of Wisconsin recently tracked a sample of 339 homeless men and women in Minneapolis over a six-month period. Between the first and second wave of the study, fully three-quarters of the sample had found conventional places to live at least once—that is, were not homeless for at least some portion of the half-year. Among the three-quarters who had been homeless and had moved into a domicile at least once, the majority then became homeless again. Finally, of those homeless at the start, "permanently" housed at least once, and then homeless at least once again, 55 percent had found yet another place to live by the end of the six-month period.[13] In other words, the most common pattern numerically revealed in these data is to be homeless at the start of the period, then to find a place to live, then to become homeless again, and then to find another place to live—two episodes of homelessness and two more or less conventional housing situations all in a six-month period.

Findings such as these expose the meaninglessness of simplistic questions such as "How many homeless people are there?" For example, the Chicago homeless study my colleagues and I did estimated that there were, on the average night in September 1985 or February 1986, about twenty-seven hundred persons sleeping in shelters or out on the streets or public places. In contrast, the same study estimated that between forty-six hundred and seven thousand persons were homeless at some time during a year. The difference between the annual and nightly estimates is a function of the turnover in the composition of the homeless in that city.[14]

No available study suggests a national total number of homeless on any given night of less than several hundred thousand, and perhaps it is enough to know that the nation's homeless are at least numerous enough to populate a medium-sized city. Although the numbers issue has been quite contentious, in a very real sense it does not matter much which estimate is closest to the truth. By any standard, all estimates point to a national disgrace.

Who Are the New Homeless?

Since 1983, forty studies of the homeless have been conducted by competent social researchers.[15] As in the 1950s and 1960s, the driving purpose behind the funding and conduct of these studies has been to provide the information necessary to design policies and programs that show promise of alleviating the pitiful conditions of the homeless. Research funds have been provided by private foundations and government agencies, among which the National Institute of Mental Health has been a major contributor.

The cities covered in these studies range across all regions of the country and include all the major metropolitan areas, as well as more than a score of smaller cities. (One study attempted to examine the rural homeless, but had little success in locating them.)[16] The cumulative knowledge about the new homeless provided through these studies is impressive. Despite differences in research methods and approaches, cities studied, professional and ideological interests of the investigators, and technical sophistication, the findings from all studies tend to converge on a common portrait. It would not be fair to say that all the important questions have been answered, but a reasonably clear understanding is now emerging of who the new homeless are, how they contrast with the general population, and how they differ from the old homeless of the 1950s.

Contrasts between the Homeless
Today and in the Past

Some of the important differences between the new homeless and the old—notably the increased numbers and visibility—have already been mentioned. Bogue estimated that only about one hundred homeless men slept out on the streets in Chicago in 1958. Theodore Caplow and Howard Bahr gave only a passing mention to the Bowery homeless sleeping out on the streets in 1964; their modest attention to this feature implies that the numbers were small. Leonard Blumberg's study of Philadelphia uncovered only sixty-four homeless persons living in the streets in 1960. In stark contrast, the recent Chicago homeless study found close to fourteen hundred homeless persons out on the streets in fall 1985 and more than five hundred in that condition in the dead of winter, early 1986. Comparably large numbers of street homeless, proportionate to community size, have been found over the past five years in studies of Los Angeles, New York, Nashville, Austin, Phoenix, Detroit, Baltimore, and Washington, D.C., among others.[17]

Thus, in the past nearly all of the old homeless managed, somehow, to find nightly shelter indoors, whereas large fractions of the new homeless population sleep in the streets or in public places, such as building lobbies and bus stations. In regard to shelter, the new homeless are clearly worse off. What is striking is that homelessness today is a more severe condition of housing deprivation than in decades past. Whatever the faults of the cubicle hotels, and there were obviously many, they at least provided more acceptable accommodations than the dormitory arrangements characteristic of today's shelters and were certainly preferable to sleeping in the streets.

Bogue's study of three decades ago also provides a point of reference regarding the increasing numbers of homeless women. Bogue estimated that women comprised perhaps 3 percent of the residents of Chicago's Skid Row; he also believed that many of them were not literally homeless but were simply living in Skid Row for their own reasons.[18] Very few women were found in the other Bowery and Skid Row studies of the era.

Yet, the Chicago homeless study found that women constituted 25 percent of the 1985–86 homeless, a proportion similar to that reported in virtually all recent studies.[19] Among those out on the street and without even emergency shelter, the proportion of women was smaller but still significant, about 18 percent. Twenty-five percent of the clients treated in the Johnson-Pew Health-Care-for-the-Homeless program were women.[20] Over a large number of recent studies in several cities, the proportion of women among the homeless varies roughly between a tenth and a third. Thus, all 1980s-era studies find women comprising a much larger proportion of the homeless than did studies undertaken before 1970.

Another contrast between the old homeless and the new is in age composition. There are very few elderly pensioners among today's homeless and virtually no Social Security pensioners. In James Wright and Eleanor Weber's study of Health-Care-for-the-Homeless clients, only 3 percent were sixty-five and over, compared to 12 percent of the national population. In the Chicago homeless study, the median age was thirty-seven, sharply contrasting with the median age of fifty found in Bogue's earlier study of that city. Indeed, today's homeless are surprisingly young; virtually all recent studies of the homeless report median ages in the low to middle thirties. Trend data over a fifteen-year period (1969–84) from the Men's Shelter in New York's Bowery suggest the median age of the homeless has been dropping by about one-half year per year for the past decade.[21]

Still another difference is provided by employment patterns and income levels. In Bogue's 1958 study, excluding the aged pensioners, over half of the homeless were employed in any given week, either full time (28 percent) or on an intermittent, part-time basis (25 percent), and almost all were employed at least for some period during a year. In contrast, among today's Chicago homeless, only 3 percent reported having a steady job, and only 30 percent worked for some period during the previous month. Correspondingly, the new homeless have less income. Bogue estimated that the median annual income of the 1958 homeless was $1,058. Our Chicago finding was a median annual income of $1,198. Correcting for the intervening inflation, the current average annual income of the Chicago homeless is equivalent to only $383 in 1958 dollars, barely a third of the actual 1958 median. Thus, the new homeless suffer a much more profound degree of economic destitution, often surviving on 40 percent or less of a poverty-level income. Today's homeless are clearly among the poorest of the poor.

A final contrast is in the ethnic composition of the new and old homeless. The old homeless were predominantly white—70 percent on the Bowery and 82 percent on Chicago's Skid Row. Among the new homeless, racial and ethnic minorities are heavily overrepresented. In the Chicago study 54 percent were black, and in the New York men's shelters more than 75 percent were black, a proportion that has been increasing since the early 1980s.[22] In most cities, other ethnic minorities, principally Hispanics and American Indians, are also found disproportionately among the homeless, although the precise ethnic mix is apparently determined by the ethnic composition of the local poverty population. In short, today, minorities are consistently overrepresented among the new homeless.[23]

Similarities between the Homeless
Then and Now

There are also some obvious continuities from the old homeless to the new. First, both groups share the condition of extreme poverty. Although the new homeless are poorer (in constant dollars), neither they nor the old homeless have (or had) incomes that would support a reasonable standard of living, whatever one takes *reasonable* to mean. The median income of today's Chicago homeless works out to less than one hundred dollars a month, or about three dollars a day, with a large proportion (18 percent) having essentially zero income. Comparably low incomes have been reported in other studies; for example, the Los Angeles study found that 46 percent of the homeless in that city had annual income less than one thousand dollars, implying a median similar to that found in Chicago.

At these income levels, even trivial expenditures loom as major expenses. For example, a single round-trip on Chicago's bus system costs $1.80, or more than half a day's median income. A night's lodging at even the cheapest flophouse costs more than five dollars, which exceeds the average daily income.[24] And, of course, the median simply marks the income received by persons at the midpoint of the income distribution; by definition, half of the homeless live on less than the median. Moreover, a homeless person's income is rarely a steady stream of three dollars and change every day. Rather, the income flow is intermittent and unpredictable, meaning that for many days in the week, or weeks in the month, or even months in the year, many of the homeless have no income.

Given the average income levels, it is certainly no mystery why the homeless are without shelter. Their incomes simply do not allow them to compete effectively in the housing market, even at the lower end. Indeed, the only way most homeless people can survive at all is to utilize the shelters for a free place to sleep, the food kitchens and soup lines for free meals, the free community health clinics and emergency rooms for medical care, and the clothing distribution depots for something to put on their backs. That the homeless survive at all is a tribute to the many charitable organizations that provide these and other essential commodities and services.

Except for the disabilities associated with old age (because there is a smaller proportion of elderly now), the new homeless and those in the past apparently share similar levels of disability—be it mental illness, physical handicap, or alcoholism. But more has been written about the homeless mentally ill than about any other aspect of the problem; Wright and Weber review about twenty pertinent studies, a list that could be readily doubled.[25] Estimates of the rate of mental illness among the homeless vary widely, from about 10 percent to more than 85 percent; most studies, however, report a figure on the order of one-third.[26] This is somewhat larger than the estimates, clustering between 15 percent and 25 percent, appearing in the literature of the 1950s and 1960s.

Many have asserted that the deinstitutionalization of the chronically mentally ill during the 1960s and 1970s was a major cause of the recent rise in homelessness.[27] No one denies that deinstitutionalization has been a contributing factor; the dispute is whether it is a major or minor one. One point frequently overlooked in these discussions is that the decanting of the mental hospital population began early in the 1960s and accelerated during the 1970s; by the start of the 1980s, almost everyone destined to be deinstitutionalized already had been. Thus, the direct effects of deinstitutionalization on homelessness have long since been diluted.

Instead, providers of services today tend to focus more on the never-institutionalized. This appropriately calls attention to the current admissions policies of our mental hospitals and the role of those policies in exacerbating the homelessness problem. Many of today's homeless mentally ill would have been admitted to mental hospitals for treatment under the commitment standards that prevailed two decades ago; today, involuntary commitment is an anathema and institutionalization a curse, and so the shelters and streets have come to substitute, at least in part, for the mental hospitals of the past.[28]

As I have already stated, the old Skid Rows also were not free of the chronically mentally ill. All the researchers of the 1950s and 1960s remarked the presence of clearly psychotic persons among the Skid Row homeless. Bogue estimated that about 20 percent of the Skid Row inhabitants were mentally ill; Blumberg found that among the Philadelphia homeless in 1960, 16 percent had been hospitalized at least once in a mental institution. Chronic mental illness has always been significant among the homeless, Skid Row having been notorious for its easy acceptance of deviant behavior of all sorts.

Although differences in diagnostic procedures confound the issue, the data from the earlier homeless studies all suggest levels of chronic mental illness that were about half those recorded from homeless studies of the 1980s. The de- and non-institutionalization processes of the past three decades have significantly contributed to the increased presence of the chronically mentally ill among today's homeless.

Physical disabilities also are widespread among the new homeless and the old. Some of the best current evidence on this score comes from the medical records of clients seen in the Johnson-Pew Health-Care-for-the-Homeless clinics. Chronic physical disorders, such as hypertension, diabetes, heart and circulatory disease, and peripheral vascular disease, are observed in 40 percent (compared to a rate of only 25 percent among urban ambulatory patients in general). "In all, poor physical health plays some direct role in the homelessness of 21 percent of the HCH clients, and is a major (or single most important) factor in the homelessness of about 13 percent. Thus, approximately one homeless adult in eight is homeless at least in major part as a result of chronically poor physical health."[29] Analysis of the deaths occurring among these clients showed that the average age at death (or in other words, the average life expectancy) of the homeless is only a bit more than fifty years.

Unfortunately, none of the studies of the "old" homeless provides comparable detail on medical conditions, although all researchers did remark on the presence of severe physical disabilities. Bogue judged that nearly half of the Skid Row homeless in 1958 had moderate to severe physical disabilities that would substantially reduce their employability, similar to the estimated 40 percent rate of chronic physical disorder reported by Wright and Weber. Bogue also found much the same mortality rates as have been found among the new homeless, namely, rates four to ten times higher than among comparable age groups in the domiciled population.

All studies of the old homeless stress the widespread prevalence of chronic alcoholism, and here, too, the new homeless are little different. Bogue found that 30 percent of his sample were heavy drinkers, defined as persons spending 25 percent or more of their income on alcohol and drinking the equivalent of six or more pints of whiskey a week. Using comparable measures, Bahr and Caplow found 36 percent to be heavy drinkers. Similar proportions were found in Minneapolis and Philadelphia around the same time.

Studies of the new homeless show similar figures. (See Table 3.1 for some of the more salient characteristics of the homeless as shown in forty empirical studies conducted between 1981 and 1988. The statistics shown are averages of findings calculated for those studies that

Table 3.1
Selected Demographic Characteristics of the Homeless[a]

	Average	*Studies*[b]
A. Gender		
Percent male	79.7%	[37]
B. Age		
Median age (years)	36.1%	[21]
Average age (years)	36.1%	[23]
C. Marital Status		
Currently unmarried	88.5%	[26]
D. Monthly Income		
Median monthly income	$164.61	[10]
Average monthly income	$ 94.55	[10]
E. Time Currently Homeless		
Average months homeless	25.6	[5]
Percent homeless for six months or more	44.6%	[13]
Percent homeless for one year or more	26.6%	[13]
F. Disabilities		
One or more mental hospital episodes	26.8%	[25]
Rated as chronic mentally ill	34.3%	[17]
Rated as alcoholic	32.7%	[15]
Reported too disabled to work	32.5%	[10]
One or more prison sentences[c]	21.3%	[12]
One or more jail sentences[c]	4.7%	[9]
Either or both prison or jail	42.1%	[16]

a. Averages of measures reported in forty empirical studies of homeless people undertaken between 1981 and 1988.
b. Number of studies in which the characteristic in question was reported.
c. Reported only for studies that distinguished between prisons and jails.

reported the measure in question.) In the Chicago homeless study, 33 percent had been in a detoxification unit at least once, indicating that one in three had had serious problems with alcohol. Recent studies in other cities give estimated rates of alcoholism ranging between 15 percent and 45 percent, with most studies clustered about an average of one-third.[30] The most methodologically sophisticated estimate, one that corrects for the tendency to underdiagnose alcohol disorders in the early visit history with a client, suggests that 38 percent of the homeless are alcoholic—16 percent of the women, 48 percent of the men.[31] The same gender difference is reported in most other studies.[32] The consensus among all studies is that about 30 to 40 percent of the new homeless are chronic alcoholics, and that the problem is more common among homeless men than women.

One variation from past practices is the growing abuse of drugs other than alcohol. Drug habits are expensive, and homeless people do not have a lot of money; still, estimates converge on about 10 percent as the rate of drug abuse among the homeless. Drug use is highest among the younger homeless and declines sharply with age.[33]

Given the emphasis that is often placed on these various disabilities as the causes of homelessness, it is important to stress that (according to the best estimates) two-thirds of the homeless are not mentally ill, three-fifths are not alcoholics, three-fifths do not suffer disabling physical disorders, and 90 percent do not abuse drugs. Hence the discussion centers in all cases on minorities—large and significant minorities, to be sure, but minorities nevertheless. Still, these disabilities tend to be cumulative; that is, a substantial majority of the new homeless have at least one and sometimes several disabling conditions. About two-thirds of the Chicago homeless had chronic physical health problems, mental health problems, or substance-abuse problems—or some combination of the three. Roughly the same was true of clients seen in the Health-Care-for-the-Homeless program.

Another point of comparability between the old and the new homeless concerns the heterogeneity of both populations. In all eras, the homeless are a mixture of some who are homeless for only short periods and others who are chronically homeless. The Skid Rows were the habitats of the chronically disabled and also points of entry for poor migrants to urban centers who rented cubicle hotel accommodations until they had established themselves and could afford conventional dwelling units. The short-term new homeless are somewhat different, often being poor people whose fortunes have temporarily taken a turn for the worse and who use the shelters to cut back on expenses until they can reestablish themselves.[34] Many of the temporary new homeless are also young-female-headed households in transition from one living arrangement to another, using the shelters for temporary residence while they establish a new household or wait for AFDC certification.

A final point of comparability is that both the old homeless and the new are socially isolated. The new homeless report few friends and intimates, and depressed levels of contact with relatives and family. There are also signs of friction between the homeless and their relatives. So extensive was the absence of social ties among the old homeless that Caplow and Bahr defined homelessness as a state of *disaffiliation,* being without enduring and supporting ties to family, friends, or kin. Disaffiliation, a condition discussed below that differentiates the homeless from others who are extremely poor but not homeless, also characterizes the new homeless.

How Do the Homeless Differ from the Extremely Poor Who Are Housed?

The foregoing comparisons between the old homeless and the new are instructive for what they tell us about how the condition of being homeless has or has not changed over time. Much additional insight can be gained by comparing the homeless with others who are just as poor but who are not homeless—the domiciled extremely poor.

It must be stressed that there are many more poor people than homeless people in this country. There are probably fewer than a million homeless people in America on any given night. In contrast, the current poverty population numbers about thirty-five million. Many of the poor are near the official poverty lines in terms of income, but many others are well below them, a group to which we shall refer as the *extremely poor.* The extremely poor also outnumber the homeless by a wide margin. In fact, the median income of poverty households in the United States works out to be just about half of the official poverty-level income: half of the poor live at or below 52 percent of the poverty level. If incomes at or below half of the poverty-level income are defined as extremely poor, then there are some seventeen million extremely poor people in the country.

It is useful to have some understanding of the quantities of income involved in being extremely poor by this definition. In 1980, the federal government defined the poverty line for a family of four as $8,414. But among poor four-person households, the 1980 median annual income was actually $4,396.

The median income for poor families yields the following calculations. First, the per-person-per-day budget: four people times 365 days in the year divided into the median income of $4,396 equals $3 per person per day, or approximately the same average daily income as was found among homeless people in Chicago in 1985–86. Suppose further that this median family spent half its income on housing: half of $4,396 divided by twelve would be $183 a month.[35] In 1983, about one-fifth of the available apartments nationwide rented for $200 a month or less, so even spending half the income on housing would put this family in the bottom quintile of the housing market. Spending half the income on housing would also leave the family with a daily budget of $1.50 a day to cover nonhousing expenses such as food, transportation, medical care, clothing, entertainment, repairs, and household furnishings.

To emphasize a critical point, there were some seventeen million people in the United States in 1980 whose living situation was as bad as or worse than the scenario sketched above, seventeen million people who, if they were lucky enough to maintain a stable residence on $200 or less per month, then had to support themselves on $1.50 a day. Given these figures for 1980 and the increased size since 1980 of the extremely poor population, it is remarkable not that we have so many homeless people in America, but that we have so *few*. To understand why some extremely poor people are homeless, one needs to understand why more of them are not.

Unfortunately, it is almost as difficult to study extremely poor people who are domiciled as it is to study the homeless.[36] The extremely poor are scattered throughout the poverty areas of our cities and do not cluster sufficiently for development of an efficient sampling plan. Some national data on the extremely poor can be obtained through the publications of the U.S. Census Bureau, but the much-discussed census undercount is a particular problem for the extremely poor population, especially in nonwhite, central-city areas. Thus, good national data on the extremely poor do not exist.

Lacking national data on the extremely poor, I have relied instead for comparison on a recent study of an important subset of the domiciled poor, specifically a survey of General Assistance (GA) recipients in Chicago conducted by Matthew Stagner and Harold Richman in 1984.[37] In Illinois, GA is a welfare program for poor persons who are not eligible for support payments under any of the various categorical support programs, such as AFDC, Social Security, or any of the disability programs. In practice, this means that GA is available for able-bodied, unattached adults whose earnings do not exceed approximately $1,800 per year and who have no significant assets. The GA payment in Illinois is $154 per month, providing an income of $1,848 per year, and it is the one benefit program in Illinois for which the majority of homeless persons are eligible.[38] Oddly enough, however, only 22 percent of the Chicago homeless in our study received GA payments.

Between 1984 and 1986, about 100,000 Chicagoans were on the Illinois GA rolls at any one time, up considerably from about 50,000 in the early 1980s. Life on GA in Illinois is a tenuous existence; the annual payment level, $1,848, works out to about $5 per day. The GA program is characterized by relatively high client turnover; the number of persons ever receiving GA over a year's time is about 150,000.

In many demographic respects, the GA clients strongly resemble the homeless; like the homeless studied in the 1985–86 Chicago survey, the GA recipients are predominately male (68 percent), black (76 percent), and unmarried (92 percent). Economically, GA clients and the homeless were also very similar: both groups had nonexistent or very small incomes, and both groups also were characterized by high unemployment and erratic employment histories.

In some demographic details, the two groups differ; for example, GA clients, with a median age of thirty-one, were about six years younger than the average Chicago homeless person. The most outstanding difference, though, is that most GA recipients are not homeless, their abysmally low incomes notwithstanding. The overwhelming majority, 92 percent, lived in conventional dwellings, with the remainder living in shelters (2 percent) or hotels or boarding houses (6 percent). Most (67 percent) of the GA recipients were living in households (as opposed to living by themselves), predominately in their parents' households. Among the one in three who lived by themselves, more than half reported that they received financial support from family, friends, and relatives; the remainder managed to survive by adding earnings from part-time, intermittent employment to their GA benefits.

Other important differences are found in the prevalence of various disabilities. Very few (1 percent) of the GA clients had ever been hospitalized for mental illness, compared to 23 percent of the homeless. Fewer were afflicted by alcoholism: 2 percent of the GA recipients mentioned alcohol problems as a reason for being unable to work, compared to 20 percent of the homeless. The GA recipients also appeared to have less contact with the criminal justice system, although the measures used in the two studies are not fully comparable. Work histories of the GA recipients were appreciably better than those of the homeless, with a majority having worked at some time during the one-year period prior to going on GA.

The above findings are critical to an understanding of homelessness in America today. GA recipients are, on average, nearly as poor as the literal homeless, and yet only 1 or 2 percent are homeless themselves. Why? Because a large portion of the GA recipients, about half the total, are living with their families, and most of the remainder receive financial support from their families. The above results make it apparent that the network of kith and kin is the last line of defense against homelessness; the homeless, in turn, are apparently those for whom this network has been destroyed in a process no doubt strongly tied to disabilities such as alcoholism or mental illness.

We shall, of course, return to these themes later. But first, it is necessary to examine some large-scale social-structural developments that have unfolded in the past decade and that provide additional important clues about the nature and magnitude of the homelessness problem in America today.

• 4 •
Structural Factors in the
Rise of the New Homeless

The Decline of Inexpensive Housing in Urban Places

In the midst of much concern about alcoholism, deinstitutionalization, physical disabilities, social disaffiliation, and the like, one must remember that homelessness is a housing problem. Homelessness on the scale seen today is in large part an outcome of the shortage of inexpensive housing for the poor, a shortage that began in the 1970s and has accelerated in the 1980s.

The decline in the low-cost housing stock has been most precipitous in the largest cities, such as New York and Los Angeles, but in varying degrees is characteristic of all cities. The Annual Housing Surveys conducted by the Census Bureau for the Department of Housing and Urban Development have recorded declines in city after city in the supply of housing that rents for 40 percent or less of poverty-level incomes. These declines ranged from 12 percent in Baltimore between 1978 and 1983 to 40 percent in Washington, D.C., between 1977 and 1981, and to 58 percent in Anaheim, California, in the same period. In twelve large cities surveyed between 1978 and 1983, the amount of inexpensive rental housing available to low-income families dropped by an average of 30 percent. One cause of the decline: federal housing programs that support the construction of public housing or provide housing subsidies for poor households have been either cut back severely or held to existing levels during the 1980s. At the same time, the number of households living at or below the poverty level in the same cities increased by 36 percent. The result of these trends in housing and income was that in the early 1980s there developed a severe shortage of housing that poor

31

households could afford without bearing excessive rent burdens. These calculations assume, incidentally, that low-income households can afford to spend 40 percent of their income on housing, a higher figure than the customary and more prudent 25 percent to 30 percent suggested by mortgage lenders.[1]

Most of the rental housing discussed above consists of multiroom units appropriate to families. In the rental housing stock that is ordinarily occupied by low-income, unattached individuals, the declines are even more precipitous. Chicago's Planning Department estimated that between 1973 and 1984, eighteen thousand single-person dwelling units (largely, rooms in SRO hotels and small apartments), amounting to 19 percent of the stock existing in 1973, were demolished or transformed for other uses.[2] The Chicago experience is not unique. Similar losses in the SRO stock have occurred in Seattle, Boston, New York, Nashville, Los Angeles, Philadelphia, and probably most other cities.[3] Indeed, a recent report indicated that between 1970 and 1985, more than half of the SRO units in downtown Los Angeles had been demolished.[4]

Earlier, I mentioned the almost complete demolition of the cubicle hotels in the 1960s and 1970s. In 1958, about eight thousand homeless were accommodated in such units in Chicago; by 1980, there were no Chicago cubicle hotels. The last two, the Star and the Major, were demolished to make room for the Presidential Apartments, a luxury complex of twelve hundred units.[5]

No one in their right mind mourns the passing of the often dirty and always inadequate cubicle accommodations, or of the SRO flophouses, or even their replacement by trendy restaurants, shops, and upscale apartment and condominium complexes. But, as James Wright and Julie Lam point out, such accommodations have always served as the "housing of last resort" for the most economically and socially marginal segments of the urban poverty population.[6] Marginal housing has largely been eliminated, but the marginal segment of the poor has not. What, then, now serves as that housing of last resort? It is transparent even to a casual analysis that the housing function once served by the cubicle and SRO hotels has been taken over by emergency shelters for the homeless and, of course, by the streets themselves.

Today, virtually no rooms in Chicago can be rented for two or three dollars a night (the current-dollar equivalent of the 1958 rents, as reported by Donald Bogue). The average SRO room cost in Chicago today (in the few SROs remaining) works out to be $195 per month, higher than the average monthly income of the Chicago homeless and also, not incidentally, higher than the average monthly GA stipend. For many of Chicago's destitute and homeless, the emergency dormitory shelters are, for all practical purposes, the only remaining alternative to sleeping in the streets. These shelters are arguably cleaner than the old cubicle and SRO hotels, but they certainly come no closer to being decent housing.

The decline of low-cost housing operates both directly and indirectly to worsen the problem of homelessness. The direct effect is obvious: if one's income is only three or four dollars a day and the cheapest possible place to live costs seven or eight dollars a day, then even the cheapest possible accommodations are out of the question. In such a case, the only alternative to homelessness would be to live with family or friends; if one were estranged from family and friends, there would be no alternative. The indirect effect is more subtle but no less important: the loss of low-income housing pushes more and more poverty households into carrying high rent burdens, which in turn leave them with proportionally less income with which to help their dependent adult members. If housing alone eats up 50 percent to 70 percent or more of the monthly income, then tough choices must be made in order to survive on the income that remains. One choice would be to turn out household members who, in better circumstances, could be allowed to stay, including, obviously, those whose drinking, extended unemployment, mental illness, drug use, or recurring troubles with the law made them disruptive or overly burdensome members of the household in the first place.

The Jewish Council on Urban Affairs' study of SRO tenants in Chicago is instructive on several points.[7] Because SRO rents are so high relative to the incomes of SRO tenants, many tenants are forced to spend very large proportions of their incomes on housing, proportions often exceeding three-quarters. These high-rent burdens mean that many tenants live on the economic "edge," and when some out-of-the-ordinary expense occurs, many SRO residents resort to the shelters or the streets where they can live free until their incomes and expenses again stabilize. The SRO study found that about one in ten of the SRO tenants had been homeless for part of the previous year, usually when they were so short of funds that they were unable to pay their room rent.

Coming at the same process from the opposite angle, both the shelter and street samples in the 1985–86 survey of the Chicago homeless claimed that they spend about 10 percent of their nights in rented rooms (presumably SRO hotel rooms). A few said they spent most nights in SRO hotels, and that we just happened to catch them in a period of temporary homelessness. Others said that they spent an occasional night or two in an SRO, perhaps when they received income windfalls. Either way, there is a considerable interchange between the homeless and the SRO populations, with the latter being a cut above the former in income (or perhaps stability of income, which is just as important).[8]

High rent burdens also force SRO tenants to "overspend" on housing and, accordingly, to skimp on other expenditures.[9] The SRO study reports that many SRO residents look to food kitchens for some or all of their meals, to free medical clinics and hospital emergency rooms for health care, and to the clothing depots for clothes. One study of soup kitchens in downtown Los Angeles found that one-third of those in the lines were renting SRO rooms.[10]

The aggregate impact of housing market dynamics on homelessness is shown dramatically in a recent analysis by William Tucker.[11] There are many deficiencies in Tucker's procedures, but some of the findings are both useful and relevant. Using HUD's estimates of the number of homeless in each of fifty cities, Tucker computed a *homelessness rate* for each city and then correlated that rate with other city characteristics.[12] The result was a fairly strong negative correlation, −.39, between housing vacancy rates in 1980 and homelessness rates in 1984. In other words, the higher the vacancy rate in a city, the lower its homelessness rate.

The critical point underscored by Tucker's analysis is that the tighter the housing market (especially the rental market) from the consumer's point of view, the greater the housing burden on poor families and the more difficult it becomes for the extremely poor to obtain or retain housing. As this becomes more and more difficult, fewer and fewer succeed, which is to say, more and more become homeless.

The Labor Market and Homelessness

Earlier, I pointed to the important labor market function of the Skid Rows of the past—in the main, providing unskilled labor to employers who needed temporary workers on an episodic basis. Much of this was seasonal work. In Chicago, Skid Row residents provided crews for summertime railroad maintenance; in Philadelphia, Skid Row men were hired over the summer by the Pennsylvania and New Jersey summer resorts. In addition, in each of the cities, a labor market existed year-round that provided temporary or spot employment on a daily basis, unloading freight cars and trucks, washing dishes in restaurants and hotels, distributing advertising flyers, and similar unskilled tasks. A major factor in the decline of the Skid Rows was the shrinkage of this casual labor market in urban economies.

This decline is carefully documented in Barrett Lee's analysis of Skid Row populations in forty-one cities during the period 1950–1970.[13] Lee shows that as the proportion of each city's labor force employed in unskilled and service occupations declined, so did the Skid Row population. In the earlier decade of the analysis, urban employers needing muscle power to wrestle with cargo apparently put up with the low productivity of Skid Row men because they could be hired as needed and at low wages. The advent of forklift tractors and other highly efficient materials-handling technology meant that casual laborers were no longer cost-effective; the declining demand for casual labor put the homeless and Skid Row out of business. The continuing lack of demand for unskilled labor still contributes to today's homelessness and helps to account for the poor employment and earnings records of the homeless. But there is another element involved, one that also helps us understand the declining average age of homeless persons. The past decade has seen a bulge in the proportion of persons between the ages of twenty and thirty-five, a direct outcome of the postwar baby boom. The consequence of this "excess" of young persons, especially males, was a depressed earnings level for young adults and an elevated unemployment rate. Richard A. Easterlin has shown that the earning power of workers under age thirty-five declined during the period between 1968 and 1984 to about 80 percent of the 1968 level, computed in constant dollars. In contrast, the real wages of workers age forty-five to fifty-five rose in the same period to 125 percent of the 1968 levels. There were similar trends in the unemployment rate. At the beginning of the period, unemployment rates for young male workers under age thirty-five were less than 5 percent but rose to a high of 15 percent in 1980 (declining to 13 percent in 1984). Unemployment among older workers, in contrast, was stable throughout the period.[14]

The point to be derived from Easterlin's analysis is that employment opportunities and earnings profiles for young men have been quite poor over the same period during which the number of homeless people increased and their average age dropped. The timing of these trends can scarcely be coincidental. In addition, the burdens imposed by poor labor market opportunities fall disproportionately upon precisely those who are overrepresented among the homeless—the disabled and minorities.

The impact of labor market and demographic trends since 1965 on women workers is more subtle. Easterlin shows that young female workers did not suffer as much as young males, although their positions in the labor market certainly showed no improvement over time. In comparison to those of young males, the earnings of young female workers did not show as sharp a decline in real dollars, and unemployment rates did not rise quite as dramatically. But there were indirect market effects that did affect women heavily, specifically, those that influenced household formation rates. (This is the issue that is referred to as the feminization of poverty: the increase in female-headed households with dependent children.)

Homeless women are younger than homeless men by about five years on the average. Almost all homeless adults accompanied by children are female.[15] The abrupt rise in female-headed households between 1968 and 1984 results in part from the uncertain economic fate of young men, especially young nonwhite men. Young men facing the economic uncertainties sketched earlier become less attractive as mates, less willing to take the chances involved in becoming a head of household, and less able to fulfill the economic role of husband and father when marriage and family formation do take place. In this respect, it is significant that almost all of the families housed in New York's welfare hotels are black or Hispanic families headed by women, that almost all of the young homeless women studied in Chicago in 1985–86 were black, and that almost all of the homeless families encountered during the study were headed by black women.[16]

• 5 •
Limits of Private, Temporary Support Systems

The Families of Failures or the Failures of Families?

It is an easy wager that there are few persons reading this essay whose family and kin would allow them to sink into literal homelessness. It is another easy wager that there are few readers who would allow that to happen to a member of their family. For most people, the initial reaction to news of a close relative who had become destitute through extended unemployment, disabling illness, severe alcoholism, or an episode of mental disturbance would be to offer financial help and even provide room for the relative in their home.

My wagers are not idle speculations. In a recent study of kinship norms, Alice Rossi and I found that almost all of a sample of metropolitan Boston adults acknowledged very strong obligations to provide financial help to their primary kin (parents, children, and siblings) in the event of illness, psychological difficulties, or unemployment.[1] But for how long would such support be given? Most would not easily begrudge providing support for a few weeks or months, or perhaps even for a year. But what if the obligation to kin required providing support for several years, and, in addition, required the sharing of already-crowded housing?

Helping out, even for long periods, might not be too hard for those who have rooms to spare in their houses or apartments and who have discretionary income left over after the monthly bills are paid. Generosity would be easier still if the dependent family member were well behaved and did nothing bizarre or in poor taste, and even more so if that person were contributing some share of his or her own support (for example, providing free day care as part of the bargain). Even so, it would be hard to put up with forever. Many people know, and admire, persons and families who have made these kinds of sacrifices for long periods of time, and thus also know of the burdens and stresses that often result.

But imagine the situation of a very low income family, living in cramped housing at the poverty level or below, on whom the responsibility for the maintenance of an unemployed adult family member has fallen. Imagine, in addition, that the family member in question has a serious alcohol or drug addiction problem, or has been in prison, or exhibits the bizarre thinking or behavior of the chronically mentally ill. Just how much assistance can the family then give? How long could they keep it up? How long should they?

It appears from the 1986–87 Chicago data that the duration of generosity under the conditions just defined is about four years, the average length of time that homeless men in the sample were unemployed before becoming homeless. During that four-year period, they were presumably supported by their families and friends—sharing housing, food, and other maintenance costs. It is perhaps axiomatic that the families and friends of homeless people are themselves very poor, with few resources to spare in any case. It is also somewhat euphemistic to talk about "families," since many of the homeless come from single-parent households, their impoverished mothers being the only ones on whom they could rely for support. Under the circumstances, maintaining a dependent, unemployed adult family member for as long as four years has to be counted as a remarkable achievement, eloquent testimony to the strength of primary kinship bonds.

There is very good, although somewhat indirect, evidence that many of the homeless have simply worn out their welcome with parents, other kin, and friends, who after an extended period of support, patience, and shared resources are exhausted. For example, the striking differences between the General Assistance population and the Chicago homeless described earlier provide such evidence. GA recipients and the homeless are almost equally destitute, but most of the GA recipients are not homeless, largely because they are subsidized by family and friends who provide housing and maintenance or supplement their income with financial aid. Why do GA recipients benefit from the generosity of their kin and friends while the homeless do not?

The interpretation is straightforward: the average GA recipient is in an early stage of his (or in a few cases her) dependency and is therefore still within the "grace period" noted above; the average homeless person is in a later stage where the grace period has expired.[2] The suggestion is that many of the GA recipients who are not able to obtain employment are on their way to becoming homeless and differ little from the homeless in other respects.

Several lines of evidence support this interpretation. First, the GA recipients are on the average six years younger than the homeless men, and by implication six years earlier in the process of dependency. The demoralizing and debilitating effects of long-term unemployment may lead to depression, mental anxieties, and alcohol and drug use, rendering even more tenuous the bonds with kin and friends. Second, whereas the average homeless man in the sample had been unemployed for four and a half years, the average male GA recipient had been unemployed for only one and a half years, a three-year differential. Both findings intimate that GA recipients are still within the acceptable period of dependency.

Also relevant, no doubt, are the comparative levels of disability. Disabilities among GA clients are much lower on every indicator in the data. Chronic mental illness, alcoholism, and physical illnesses are less prevalent by several magnitudes among GA recipients than among the homeless. The relative absence of disabilities among GA recipients compared to the homeless may also mean that their grace period is longer; they demand fewer resources—both economic and emotional—and therefore can be put up for longer periods.

The Chicago study also produced one direct piece of evidence on these points. One question sequence asked whether recipients would like to return to their families, and if so, whether they felt they would be taken back in. Most homeless men said they would like to return, but most also knew they would not be welcome. The women, in contrast, did not wish to return in the first place, many of them having fled domestic situations so unacceptable that a life of homelessness became the preferred alternative.

The line of reasoning pursued above applies only to those who have living primary kin who have taken responsibility for them. There is some evidence from Irving Piliavin and Michael Sosin's study of homeless in Minneapolis that many of the homeless were reared in foster homes and hence may have no primary kin upon which they could rely.[3] There are many reasons for foster home placement of children, including parental mortality, court judgment of parental neglect, and parental request. Whatever the cause, those without any willing and able primary kin are particularly vulnerable to becoming homeless.

The Erosion of People's Ability to Help

The preceding analysis showed that a large share of the support of extremely poor unattached adults is borne by poverty-stricken households who stretch their meager resources to provide housing and maintenance to their dependent adult children and, sometimes, to friends. The extent to which these burdens have come to rest on the shoulders of poor families can be seen in trends in the numbers of young adults who live with their parents, especially among the poor. National data indicate that young black men are especially likely to live in their parental households. According to the Census Bureau, in 1970, 39 percent of both black and white men, aged eighteen to twenty-nine, lived with their parents. By 1984, 54 percent of young black men lived with their parents, while only 41 percent of whites of comparable age did so.

Direct evidence of the increased burdens on poor households indicated in these trends is difficult to come by, since information is not available on the specific households from which the homeless come. Because the households are largely low-income, however, one can assume that many are assisted by welfare, in particular, AFDC. Some indication of the declining economic position of the poor can therefore be found by looking at trends in the constant-dollar values of welfare and related transfer payments between 1968 and 1985 (see Table 5.1). For most programs, the trend is strongly downward.

Although Social Security payments actually increased by 162 percent from 1968 to 1984 (in constant dollars) and most other benefit programs under Social Security remained fairly steady in value, there were drastic declines in the constant-dollar values of both AFDC and GA payments over the same period. On the national level, AFDC payments in 1985 were worth only 63 percent of their 1968 value. Illinois AFDC payments declined to 53 percent of 1968 value in the same period. An even more drastic decline occurred in Illinois' GA payments, the programs most readily available to homeless persons and to the unattached. In 1985, GA payments in Illinois were worth only 48 percent of their 1968 value. The major loss of value in both AFDC and GA occurred between 1975 and 1980, reflecting the ravages of inflation and the evident reluctance of policymakers to compensate for inflation by raising payment levels.[4]

Quite clearly, poor families dependent on AFDC or GA entered the decade of the 1980s with a considerably diminished financial capacity, and thus, a much-reduced ability to provide help to their dependent adult relatives. Trends in the living arrangements of young men, as noted earlier, have obviously added to the economic strains. At some point (with the precise point no doubt highly variable across households), the strains would be too much; the demands on meager incomes would exceed the carrying capacity of those incomes. In nature, the result of an analogous situation is that the weakest and most dependent are kicked

Table 5.1
Constant-Dollar[a] Average Monthly Transfer Payments, 1968–85
Illinois and National Averages

National Monthly Average Payments (1985 Dollars) Transfer Program	*1968*	*1975*	*1980*	*1985*
Old Age Retirement	$295	$414	$446	$479
Disability	[b]	$452	$485	$484
Widows/Orphans	[b]	$388	$406	$433
Supplemental Security Income for the Aged	$217	$182	$167	$164
SSI for the Blind	$285	$294	$278	$274
SSI for Disability	$257	$282	$259	$261
AFDC	$520	$464	$366	$325

Illinois Monthly Average Payments (1985 Dollars) Transfer Program	*1968*	*1975*	*1980*	*1985*
Old Age Retirement	$311	$434	$474	$511
Disability	[b]	[c]	$506	$505
Widows/Orphans	[b]	[c]	$435	$466
Supplemental Security Income for the Aged	$204	[c]	$159	$100
SSI for the Blind	$263	[c]	$108	[c]
SSI for Disability	$269	[c]	$246	$142
AFDC	$644	$568	$362	$342
General Assistance	$322	[c]	[c]	$154

[a] Shown in 1985 dollars. Consumer Price Index used as a deflator. *Sources: Social Security Bulletin, Annual Statistics Supplement, 1986; Social Security Bulletin, June 1986; Statistical Abstract of the United States, 1987, 1981, 1976, 1969;* Illinois Department of Public Aid.
[b] Program not in place.
[c] Data not available for these years in sources.

from the nest. Is the upsurge of homelessness in the major cities any different?

There is no doubt that the much-diminished value of AFDC payments has contributed directly to the appearance and rise of female-headed households among the homeless population. Female-headed households dependent on AFDC would find it difficult or impossible to cover their housing and other expenses on payment levels that are clearly lower than the rents typically charged for small apartments. AFDC-dependent mothers live exceedingly close to financial disaster; any unanticipated expense could create a crisis. Given the current purchasing power of the average AFDC payment, it is no wonder that many young-female-headed households often become literally homeless. Indeed, the Massachusetts courts have recently compared the average AFDC payment to the average rents in Boston and concluded that the payment level must be contributing directly to the rise of homelessness.[5]

The similarly precipitous drop in the dollar value of GA payments has also had implications for homelessness. General Assistance payments in 1968 were generous enough at least to cover the rent for SRO rooms, with even a bit left over, perhaps, for other expenses. In addition, an unattached adult male on GA would have had enough income in 1968 from his benefits to make a significant contribution to the income of his parental household, if that were his living situation. He might still have been dependent on parental assistance, but not completely so. In contrast, by 1985, the value of GA payments had been more than cut in half; as a result, a GA client could neither make significant contributions to a host household nor get by on his or her own. While the purchasing power of GA payments in 1968 was at least somewhere close to the actual survival costs for a single person, by 1985 it was not.[6]

Table 5.1 also helps explain why, in sharp contrast to previous decades, so few aged persons can be found among the homeless of the 1980s. As mentioned earlier, old-age Social Security benefits increased greatly in purchasing power from 1968 to 1985, a result of favorable changes in the benefit levels in 1972 and the subsequent indexing of the benefit levels to the Consumer Price Index. Indeed, in 1968, the dollar value of average old-age pensions in Illinois was slightly below the value of GA payments; by 1985, the average old-age pension had increased in purchasing power by 162 percent while the average GA stipend had declined—in 1985 the old-age pension was 3.3 times the value of GA. Note also that the absolute dollar amount of the average old-age pension in 1985, $511, would be sufficient to rent accommodations in the conventional housing market, and certainly sufficient for rentals in sub-sidized senior citizens' housing developments.

The sharply enhanced economic well-being of the elderly is one of the great political success stories of the twentieth century. Throughout most of the century, the elderly were greatly overrepresented among the poor; today, for the first time in our history, the poverty rate for persons aged sixty-five and over is less than that of the rest of the population. How this was accomplished says a lot about how the problem of homelessness will have to be solved, if indeed it ever is. The government virtually wiped out poverty among the aged by spending and continuing to spend an enormous amount of money. Public spending on the elderly, through Social Security pensions, Medicare, and housing subsidies, literally dwarfs every other item in the federal human services budget.[7]

• 6 •
What Can Be Done?

The important questions to be asked, before deciding on programs to address the problem of homelessness, are: Why are some kinds of people more likely than others to be homeless? And why has homelessness increased so sharply over the past decade?

It is important, first, to distinguish between the short-term (episodically) homeless—the apparent majority—and the long-term (chronically) homeless. Most of what I have to say concerns the latter group, the most seriously disadvantaged and the core of the homelessness problem. The short-term homeless consist primarily of persons living in poverty whose month-to-month finances are precarious and for whom short-term reversals of fortune result in episodes of homelessness of varying severity and duration. There is evidence that the episodically homeless comprise the majority of homeless persons today: across the thirteen homelessness studies in which the length of time of homelessness was ascertained, an average of 55 percent had been homeless for less than six months.[1]

The dynamics of episodic homelessness are distressingly straightforward. So long as there is a poverty population whose incomes put them on the economic edge, there will be people who fall, periodically, over that edge and into a state of homelessness. The solution is to develop provisions in the social welfare system that would protect against short-term economic difficulties.

What of the chronically homeless, the one in four who has been homeless for two or more years and who appears likely to continue in that condition for a much longer period? The distinguishing characteristics of the long-term homeless are their extraordinarily high levels of

45

disabilities* of all sorts, incapacities that impair their earning power, diminish their employment prospects, and reduce their acceptance by families, kin, and friends. These are the persons most strongly and directly affected by shortages of unskilled positions in the labor force, by the loss of inexpensive housing, and by declines in the economic fortunes of their social networks. Under these unfavorable conditions, unattached persons afflicted with disabilities have an increasingly difficult time living on their own; at the same time, these disabilities also make them less tolerable as adult dependents in parental households, particularly as the living conditions of poor households deteriorate.

Pointing to the high level of disability among the chronically homeless as their distinguishing characteristic is not an instance of blaming the victim. It is merely to explain that the disabled (as defined here) are the most vulnerable to perverse macrolevel social forces—the loss of low-income housing and declining demand for unskilled labor. If anything, the blame for homelessness lies on a society whose political economy (housing market, labor market, and welfare system) creates a housing "game" that more and more poor people are destined to lose. It is no surprise, surely, that the losers tend to be the most vulnerable segments of the poverty population.

What, then, is to be done? The very impressive increase in researchers' knowledge of homelessness in the past five years does not suggest any quick fixes or instant remedies. Homelessness in the larger sense may well be here for decades and may never be totally erased, largely because the problem results, as noted, from large-scale societal developments that are not likely to be rolled back. Still, being able to assure that no one involuntarily goes without nightly shelter, even if that shelter may not fulfill all our ideal definitions of *home,* is a realistic aspiration. And it is also a reasonable goal to reduce to the absolute minimum the number of individuals and families whose living situations fall short of the security, stability, safety, and privacy that are associated with the larger meaning of *home.*

---

* Please note: *disabled* in this context is meant to include any condition that appreciably impairs a person's ability to make minimally successful connections with the labor market and form mutually satisfactory relationships with family and friends. This definition includes much that goes beyond the usual meaning of *disability;* for example, it includes criminal records that interfere with employment chances, or chronic problems with drinking, as well as the more customary physical and psychiatric impairments that are ordinarily included in the concept.

It is thus useful to divide what needs to be done into two parts: first, the policy changes needed to deal with the short-term problem, to ameliorate the condition of the current homeless; and second, policy changes necessary to deal with the long-term problem, to mitigate the risk of becoming homeless in the first place.

Short-term Remedies

Under short-term remedies are included all measures that do not require drastic overhauls of the current institutions of society. One important set of short-term remedies is to be found in the reform of existing social welfare programs. There is much leverage on the problem to be had here, simply because there is abundant evidence that the homeless are frequently individuals who have slipped through the loose weave of the existing social welfare safety net. Almost all recent research has shown that relatively few homeless participate even in welfare programs for which they would appear to be eligible by virtue of their financial plight and disabilities.[2]

Relatively few of the homeless receive Social Security Disability Income or Supplemental Security Income payments, food stamps, or AFDC payments, or participate in state General Assistance programs where they are available. In the Chicago study, for example, almost all of the homeless were eligible for one or another of the more generous benefit programs. However, only 22 percent received GA payments, less than 7 percent received SSI, less than 7 percent received SSDI, and a little more than 6 percent received AFDC.[3]

It is important to recognize that the low participation rate of the homeless in many of these programs, especially those with the more generous payments, results in part from the fact that those who do participate receive sufficient income to find some kind of shelter. This is so particularly for SSDI: there are few SSDI participants among the homeless because the program provides enough money (the average payment in Illinois is $504 per month) to afford the rent for an SRO hotel room or a cheap apartment. Even the most poorly supported program, GA, provides more income per month ($154) than the median income of all homeless ($100), which is to say that the average homeless person not already receiving GA could significantly increase his or her income through a GA benefit. There are no doubt many economically marginal persons in Chicago and elsewhere who patch together intermittent jobs and GA welfare payments and then find their way into SROs and rooming houses.

That said, low levels of participation in benefit programs also reflect the difficulties that many homeless people experience connecting with the welfare system and, once connected, in remaining on the rolls. Although the application process for many programs is not extremely difficult, homeless persons often find it hard to negotiate the several interviews, submission of affidavits, and other program requirements. Because the homeless have very little standing as citizens and are often unable to lodge effective complaints, they are especially vulnerable to being cut off when budget crunches lead welfare administrations to look for persons whom they may safely terminate.

Data from the Chicago study show dramatically the difficulties homeless people experience with the welfare system. Among the Chicago homeless, more than 70 percent of those eligible for GA said they had applied for benefits at one time or another, but a majority had either been turned down or accepted but later terminated. Those eligible for AFDC had had similar experiences: of those determined to be eligible, almost all (96 percent) said they had applied for AFDC, but only 7 percent were currently receiving benefits. The remainder had been turned down or accepted but later terminated. The reasons given in the welfare records for termination were overwhelmingly technical violations, consisting of such things as failure to appear at appointments and failure to register at employment agencies.

Solving the problem of low levels of welfare participation among the homeless can be accomplished in substantial part by welfare agencies without legislative authorization changes. An aggressive outreach program to enroll as many as are eligible in disability and public welfare programs would significantly raise the income levels of homeless persons and enable a few of them to leave that condition. In addition, the welfare agencies should review their practices regarding termination of benefits for technical reasons and make reasonable allowances for the unique difficulties homeless persons face. Keeping appointments is not easy if you have neither an appointment book nor a watch.

Raising levels of welfare participation is a first step, but unless benefit levels are raised (as discussed below), the additional income will not normally enable the homeless to live in conventional dwelling units or SROs.

Participation is also relatively low in in-kind benefit programs such as Food Stamps or Medicaid. In many states, Medicaid eligibility is tied to income-transfer programs, and hence participation rates will rise with increased enrollment in welfare programs. Other in-kind programs are more problematic, in particular, the Food Stamp program. Changes in Food Stamp regulations are needed to allow the use of food stamps under congregate living conditions. In particular, it should be possible for food kitchens, shelters, and perhaps even restaurants to utilize the food stamps of their clients; this would substantially increase the practical utility of food stamps to homeless persons and provide additional funds to those agencies. Similar changes are also needed in housing subsidies, such as those provided under Section VIII of the current Housing Act, to enable the use of these subsidies in renting SRO or similar accommodations.

A second short-term measure would be to remove the most severely disabled from the shelters and the streets and move them into total-care institutions. In particular, this means that many of the chronically mentally ill homeless should be removed to environments where they can be given highly supervised supportive care; for some of the most severely impaired, this may require "removal" to the large state mental hospitals. This will strike many civil libertarians as a step backward, but the principle embodied in deinstitutionalization is that the mentally ill should be treated in the least restrictive environment "consistent with their ability to function" without harm to themselves and others. Living on the streets is certainly the least restrictive environment imaginable, but it is not an environment that provides for any sensible regimen of medication or care, and it is also not consistent with their ability to function. "Abandonment," as James Wright has put it, "is not liberation."

For the most severely deteriorated of the chronically mentally ill, those whose behavior is intentionally or unintentionally self-destructive, institutionalization is probably the only sensible alternative to a miserable life and an early death. If this suggestion is considered a step backward in civil liberties for the mentally ill, it is a necessary step backward. Proper and zealous guarding of someone's civil rights cannot mean leaving that person in a condition that poses immediate and considerable physical risk; if so, the concept of civil rights is stripped of all practical meaning. After several decades of deinstitutionalization and restricted institutionalization, it must also be recognized that implementing this recommendation may require upgrading and expanding the mental hospital system, especially in those states with insufficient hospital capacities.

Implementing this recommended policy would require two important changes in current policy: First, hospital releases of the chronically mentally ill should be undertaken only when there are assurances that supportive living arrangements are available for the released patient. Second, it must be made easier to commit chronically mentally ill persons when they are unable to care for themselves outside an institutional context.

The first recommendation means that a patient with a chronic mental illness should not be released unless there are kin who are willing and able to provide shelter for the patient or unless there is a supervised living accommodation available. To make it easier for such arrangements to be established, I recommend that the patient be enrolled in some disability payment program before discharge and that the receiving household or nonhospital living accommodation be assigned a reasonable portion of those payments. The cost of such a program would not be excessive. Assuming that about a third of the current homeless would eventually find their way into this program, annual costs would be about $600 million, assuming monthly disability stipends of five hundred dollars and a population of one hundred thousand chronically mentally ill homeless persons.

The second recommendation involves making it easier for kin, social agencies, and the police to bring a person who is acting in a bizarre manner, is incoherent, or is neglecting to care for himself or herself to the courts for psychiatric evaluation and subsequently for involuntary commitment, if the complaints are sustained. Under present practices there are many incentives for the courts to "plea-bargain" with such persons brought before them, trading voluntary (and limited) commitment for the more extensive procedure involved in involuntary (and usually longer-term) commitment. The extensive use of such plea bargaining in Illinois has led to the hospitals serving as short-term residential accommodations where little therapy can be provided.[4] My recommendation is that patients, whether voluntarily or involuntarily committed, be treated the same when it comes to discharge, but that at the point of discharge the provisions noted above under the first recommendation be followed.

A third short-term measure would be to maintain and possibly improve the financial support given to existing shelters, and where necessary, to add new shelters. In many cities, even reasonable and conservative estimates of the number of homeless persons show that there are twice as many homeless as there are existing shelter beds. In addition, these emergency shelter dormitories are far from satisfactory accommodations in the best of cases, and there is also the danger that a shelter "industry" may develop that acquires a strong stake in the permanent existence of what should be rightly construed as temporary measures.

It is a safe bet that there are few large urban centers in which shelter capacities come close to being adequate for the current numbers of homeless. Yet there is some evidence that the shelters are not used to their capacities: the Chicago study found the shelters available in winter (February 1986) used only to 80 percent of capacity. Those shelters that anyone would judge as better in providing more privacy and greater safety came closer to being at full capacity than the more open and less safe dormitory accommodations provided by the larger shelters. I believe that it says something about the conditions of our shelters when one-third to one-half of the homeless are out on the streets and in public places in the dead of Chicago's winters while shelter capacity goes unused. It is also important to note that some shelters reject the most disabled as clients,[5] and that some of the homeless have greater than justified fears about their personal safety within the shelters.

The need for emergency overnight shelter clearly offsets whatever misgivings the homeless may have about shelters as accommodations. A sensible policy may be to make the subsidies for shelters proportional to the quality of the accommodations given, thereby providing incentives to upgrade to more private and safer facilities. Ironically, though, if all shelters were brought up to the quality levels of the best of them, the outcome might be a charity- and public-funds-subsidized version of the better SRO hotels.

Long-term Policy Recommendations

In the long term, the solutions to homelessness will be policies that compensate for the failures and inadequacies of the housing and labor markets and those of our social welfare system. An important long-term goal will have to be the improvement of the employment experience of young minority males. There can be little doubt that the current group of homeless young males is the result of the past two decades of catastrophically high unemployment rates for young minority males. Most of the homeless young men have not held steady jobs for five years, and some have never been employed. To reduce homelessness among young men in their thirties requires that we provide them with employment much earlier in the course of their lives, in late adolescence and in their early twenties.

The major thrust of our policies for reducing unemployment among minority youths has been aimed at improving the quality of their job skills, thereby improving their employment prospects in the existing labor market. There have been several problems with our job-training programs over the past few decades. First of all, the programs have not been targeted enough to young adults. If the nation wants to avoid having a large group of chronically unemployed men in their thirties, it needs to work on improving the employment prospects of young men shortly after they finish their education. Second, given the experience with job-training and supported-work programs over the past two decades, it is hard to be optimistic about using such programs to compensate for the failure of the labor market to provide employment opportunities. On completion of these programs, participants frequently do not have any better chance to be employed or earn higher wages than those who did not participate. There is an extensive literature on the evaluation of job-training and supported-work programs; the record is one of failure in almost all cases.[6]

Most notable are the disappointing results of the extremely impressive Supported Work Experiment conducted by the Manpower Demonstration Research Corporation (MDRC),[7] even though the program was aimed at persons who were beyond late adolescence and in early adulthood. The experiment provided instruction in job deportment, job search, and job skills to drug users, released prisoners, AFDC recipients, and the chronically unemployed—in short, persons with the worst labor market prospects. The training was accompanied by paid employment in environments that made increasing performance demands over time. In comparison to randomly selected control groups who did not participate in MDRC's program, no detectable improvement occurred for male participants. The experiences with female participants, in contrast, were more positive. Women participants in the program had lower unemployment and higher earnings after training than did the controls.

Evaluations of a variety of other job-training programs have produced similarly dismal findings in almost all cases. Apparently, fiddling with the supply side of the labor market accomplishes very little in the way of long-term improvements in employment or earnings for young adults.

Interventions dealing with the demand side of the labor market have also been disappointing, although they do show some net public benefits. For example, although the Comprehensive Employment and Training Act (CETA) program started under President Jimmy Carter did not materially improve the subsequent labor market performances of its clients, it did provide significant amounts of employment to the otherwise unemployed. CETA also augmented the labor supply available to local and state governments, and made possible increased public services.

If the private labor market is unable to provide sufficient employment opportunities to able young people, then the nation may have to resort to public-sector employment. Indeed, some of the most popular welfare programs in U.S. history have been, in essence, public employment programs—for example, the Civilian Conservation Corps of the Great Depression, the Job Corps, the Peace Corps, and VISTA (Volunteers in Service to America). The Works Progress Administration public employment programs of the Great Depression did not get as good a hearing in the press, but their accomplishments in the way of public works can still be seen all over the country in public buildings, park improvements, and so forth.

When the labor market fails to provide employment to young people, an appropriate remedy is to provide public employment. At the moment the only public employment program widely available to young people is the armed forces, providing employment and training opportunities that have been very attractive to minority young men. There is a need for civilian equivalents to the armed forces, providing jobs that produce transferable skills and that also increase the quantity and quality of public facilities. I hesitate to recommend specific programs, but there is no dearth of urban public facilities in need of augmentation and refurbishing, from our streets to our libraries and schools. There also are many public services needing additional personnel, ranging from public transportation to tax collection.

There are many potential advantages to public employment programs, especially in contrast to income maintenance programs. Public employment programs are preferable in terms of human values because they mitigate both the demoralizing effects of unemployment and the stigma of welfare. These are programs that provide earned income and job activities to people who otherwise would have neither. The overhead costs of these programs might well exceed the corresponding costs of simple transfer-payment programs, but there are benefits to participants that cannot be obtained through straight cash payouts: something productive to do with one's time, and consequent self-worth. A most attractive feature is that such programs can also increase the amount and quality of public facilities.

Demography, it is said, is destiny, and therein lies some optimism. The demographic changes that can be anticipated over the next decade will strongly improve the labor market position of young males. The postwar baby boom that has flooded the labor market with young people, depressing both real wages and employment prospects, will have subsided within the next four or five years. Beginning in the early 1990s, there will be fewer young people entering the labor market, and that will improve prospects for all subsequent cohorts.[8] Despite the improved prospects that such demographic changes promise to bring, there will still be greater unemployment among minority youths than among others.

Recommendations concerning the housing market can be stated more optimistically. Clearly, the housing market has failed to provide for the special needs of unattached poor persons. The program of federal housing subsidies for the elderly (coupled with rising benefit levels for old-age pensioners) has largely succeeded in removing the aged from the ranks of the homeless; and if the nation can do it for the aged, then it can certainly do the same for the young.

An effective housing program along these lines would attempt to preserve and upgrade existing housing as well as add new housing stock. In at least one city, Los Angeles, a nonprofit corporation has been formed to purchase, rehabilitate, and manage SRO hotels that come on the market. How successful this will be in providing clean, safe, and decent living accommodations at reasonable rentals is yet to be seen, but the promise is clearly there.[9]

In the past, society has shown more concern for the housing problems of unattached persons. In the first part of this century, the Young Men's Christian Association and the Young Women's Christian Association built residential hotels in most urban places in order to provide wholesome and affordable housing for single men and women.[10] Whether the "Ys" or an equivalent organization could do it again today is an open question. Most likely, some form of government subsidy would be necessary. Furthermore, the Y hotels never aspired to dominate the housing market: inexpensive, commercial SRO hotels and rooming houses provided most of the housing for unattached persons. Governmental policies should also be directed at bolstering what remains of this segment of the low-rent urban housing stock.

One problem that has been encountered in many cities in both the rehabilitation of existing housing and the construction of new low-income units is that local building codes and zoning restrictions are often very strict, making many such projects economically unfeasible. Substantial renovations of SRO hotels in Los Angeles, for example, require retrofitting the structures to contemporary seismic safety standards. Whether the building codes in question are sensible regulations that substantially promote the public welfare is beyond the scope of this essay. In any event, their existence may mean that the provision of adequate amounts of low-cost housing will be expensive.[11]

Phasing out emergency shelters as quickly as new housing programs provide sufficient accommodations for unattached persons should also be a public policy priority. The prospect that dormitory living for the unattached poor will soon become a fixed feature of the cities is very real. There are many precedents for programs living far beyond their usefulness as they evolve into self-serving bureaucracies with greater stakes in self-preservation than in fulfilling a function. Currently, there is nothing but the streets and public places that compete for the clients of the shelters. As serious competitors appear on the scene, emergency shelters should disappear gracefully.

A final set of recommendations concerns the holes in the social welfare safety net. At present, benefit programs provide mainly for the aged, for the families of dependent children, and for those who have recognized, "traditional" disabilities—such as blindness or partial paralysis. Aging people, dependent children, and the physically disabled arouse considerable sympathy on the part of legislatures and the larger public, who respond magnanimously to the needs of these groups. The nation has yet to fully recognize other forms of disability that are equally damaging to an individual's capacity to participate fully in our society, especially in the labor force.

The disabilities of chronic mental illnesses are recognized in our disability benefit programs, but with some ambivalence. In comparison to blindness or paralysis, chronic mental illness is less easily recognized as a disability, leading to discretionary actions that may often deny benefits to persons in need. Indeed, the very definition of mental illness is fuzzy, with honest disagreements about classification often arising among professionals. Yet, if the chronically mentally ill are to live outside of institutions in reasonably safe and decent accommodations, government must ensure that they are routinely included and more generously maintained within our disability support mechanisms. Indeed, the deinstitutionalization movement of the 1960s and 1970s was undertaken on the assumption that the chronically mentally ill would be supported in the community by either SSI or SSDI payments, an expectation that was only weakly realized.[12]

Concerning substance abuse as a disabling condition, our ambivalence is even greater. Thanks to long-term campaigns by Alcoholics Anonymous and similar groups, there is increasing acceptance of the notion that alcoholism is a disease. Persuaded by this redefinition, legislatures have largely decriminalized public drunkenness, and have attempted to substitute detoxification for arrest.

The definition of disability should be extended to include the more advanced stages of alcoholism as a condition requiring maintenance. A counterargument is that such a change would only serve as an incentive for persons to become more careless in their drinking habits. Everyone would likely recognize that no one deliberately becomes paraplegic in order to obtain disability entitlements, but there may be an assumption that low-income drinkers might well increase or prolong their drinking if the end result was a generous monthly check. However, it would be difficult to hold to that counterargument in the face of knowledge about the long-term consequences of severe alcoholism: no one could reasonably believe that the ravages of that disease could be compensated for by a monthly check, no matter how generous. Chronic alcoholics are as surely and severely disabled by their condition as is any blind or paralyzed person. The costs of such an extension of the disability program may be more expensive than full extension to cover the mentally ill: assuming one hundred thousand advanced alcoholics among the homeless and another five hundred thousand in the domiciled population, a program providing $500 a month would cost $3.5 billion in benefits alone. Given the public policy concern that benefits to severe chronic alcoholics might increase their alcohol intake, a major portion of the benefits might be paid directly to persons or institutions providing care for the beneficiaries—their families, detoxification centers, or supervised living environments.

Other aspects of the welfare system also need correction. Our society consistently underestimates the importance of income, especially to the poor, often mistaking the effects of poverty for the effects of personal deficiencies. Nothing seemed more dismal to those researching the old Skid Rows in the 1960s than the apparent and utter hopelessness of the aged pensioners found there. Few, if any, advocated raising old-age pensions to ameliorate their inadequate living conditions. Yet, as the value of old-age pensions rose in the subsequent decades, the drop in the number and proportion of aged persons among the homeless was dramatic. Provided with a reasonable level of income, the generations who became elderly in the 1970s and 1980s were spared the fate of becoming homeless.

The lesson of what higher benefits accomplished for the aged may be applied to many other categories of today's homeless population. I have already documented the severe deterioration in AFDC and GA benefits over the past two decades. Inflation has lowered the real value of these payments to the point where recipients are not raised to a level that is even near the poverty level. This deterioration in support for families and individuals undoubtedly increased homelessness and changed the composition of the homeless population. Government creates homelessness and shelter dependency when it provides too little money even to pay the rent. Society creates more homelessness by placing the burden on poor families to provide support for their unemployed—sometimes unemployable—adult members. We foster long-term shelter dependency when we fail to provide long-term unemployed, single, unattached persons with enough money to rent better accommodations. All of these changes have shifted the age structure of the homeless downward and have increased the proportion of minorities among the homeless.

There are two remedies for these problems. The first is as simple to implement as it is expensive: restore the value of welfare benefits that have been so seriously eroded by inflation over the past twenty years. This would restore the ability of many among the poor to cope more effectively with the housing market. It is a shameful irony that New York's welfare department pays three to four times the going rent for low-cost apartments to welfare hotels to house single-parent families who are homeless because they cannot rent apartments on their inadequate welfare benefits.

There is some substantive evidence that the American public would favor such a move. In a 1986 national survey conducted by the National Opinion Research Center, a sample-survey research unit affiliated with the University of Chicago, respondents favored awarding to single-parent families benefits that were several times those currently in place.[13] Although the average payment under AFDC was $325 per month in 1985, survey respondents awarded $1,152 per month to AFDC-eligible families, more than 3.5 times the current benefit level. The American public apparently understands inflation and its consequences better than do its legislators.

Current AFDC expenditures run about $15 billion annually. Restoring the ravages of inflation over the past two decades would involve a 60 percent increase to $24 billion. Offsetting some of these costs are the savings to be realized by the resulting improved health status of both mothers and children, the bolstering of the lower end of the rental housing market by firming up demand, and the increased expenditures for other consumer goods.

The second remedy is more difficult because it entails subsidies for categories of families and persons that have not historically received welfare support. The recommendation is to provide direct support to families who subsidize their destitute, unattached adult members—in effect, *Aid to Families with Dependent Adults*. The purpose of such a program is obvious: to help poor families provide housing, food, and other amenities to their adult members who cannot support themselves. This might take a variety of forms. For example, if the GA payment to a destitute adult is, say, three hundred dollars per month, an additional payment could be provided directly to any primary kin providing a home to that adult. Another alternative is to split benefit payments, part going to the recipient and part going to caretakers. The reader may recall that similar provisions were proposed elsewhere in this paper, to be attached to disability benefit programs. To assure that government spending for this would be concentrated on poor households, the benefit payments to households should be taxed as income.

It would be difficult to exaggerate the difficulties of defining such a program and administering it. Benefit programs traditionally have been addressed to persons either before maturity or beyond ordinary working years. Indeed, the very title of AFDC emphasizes that the benefits are being made for the sake of the children involved, underemphasizing the fact that support for adults in their working years is also being supplied. The program here has as its target adults in their working years who do not have responsibility for children, a group that society has not been generous to in the past. However, legislators and the public might react with sympathy for the families who have taken on the burdens of supporting dependent adults and would look with more sympathy on a program that would help to ease those burdens.

The extent of adult dependency is surprisingly large. In 1987, the Current Population Survey estimated that there were some 4.9 million unmarried, childless persons between the ages of twenty-two and fifty-nine who were neither students nor living on farms and whose 1986 incomes were under four thousand dollars. Three million earned less than two thousand dollars. The majority (60 percent) lived with parents or siblings, the remainder either alone (20 percent) or with nonrelatives (20 percent).[14] Many of these unattached adults were only temporarily destitute: in March 1987, when the survey was conducted, a third were employed.

If the eligibility requirements of the program are set so that an unattached adult must have an income under four thousand dollars for at least eighteen months before becoming eligible, and that as many as 1 million would probably be eligible for benefits under disability programs, then approximately 2–2.5 million would likely qualify. Assuming benefits that amounted to six thousand dollars per year or five hundred dollars per month, the benefit payments would amount to $12 to $15 billion annually. The net cost would be offset to some degree by the increased tax liabilities of the host households.

A critical point of the proposal is that the benefits be shared between the unattached person and that person's family if they share a household. The immediate problem encountered is the need to define which kinship relationships are "family": certainly parents and children would qualify, as would siblings. More distant kin, such as grandparents and parents' siblings, are problematic. I suggest that family be narrowly confined to parents, children, and siblings, including step- or foster versions. Another difficulty surrounds how to split and deliver the payments, and that must be left to the experts in the design of payment systems.

Finally, there is the problem of how to strip such a benefit system of unintended disincentives. For example, the system should encourage dependent adults to become employed, possibly by tapering off payments to beneficiaries rather than abruptly terminating them when they become employed. The program also ought to encourage the formation of new households, but only if there is some assurance that the new household will not simply become a beneficiary of some other program. Of course, programs of this kind are difficult to administer and subject to abuse, but if we abandoned all programs of which that might be said, we would never accomplish anything.

• 7 •
Conclusions

It is important to summarize what has been learned about homelessness from the social research of the past several years before examining what that knowledge implies about possible solutions.

The following points deserve recapitulation:

- The old homeless were concentrated in a few segregated districts in the large cities. The new homeless tend to be dispersed more widely over the urban landscape, making extreme poverty and homelessness far more visible.
- The new homeless are strikingly worse off than the old homeless. However inadequate the old cubicle hotels may have been, they still provided a modicum of shelter. A majority of the new homeless are completely without shelter, and the remainder are provided shelter in unsatisfactory dormitory accommodations. Urban housing markets have been stripped of inexpensive housing, especially for unattached persons and for recently formed poor households. While much has been done to provide refurbished downtown housing for young urban professionals, little or nothing is provided for the young urban poor. Furthermore, however poor the old homeless may have been, their income levels were several magnitudes above those of the new homeless (in constant dollars).
- The old homeless were almost all unattached men; many were old men at the end of their working lives. The prospects for rehabilitation, for many, were slight. In contrast, the new homeless include a large contingent of women, many with their children. Also, the new homeless are composed largely of younger persons who would ordinarily be employed full time. The prospects of reestablishing tradi-

tional life-course trajectories appear to be better for some of the new homeless than they would have been for the old.

• The old homeless had a niche within the social ecology of the labor market, furnishing labor for seasonal activities or for short-term, low-skilled jobs. The market for such jobs has shrunk considerably with the advent of new technologies. The new homeless—unskilled and often disabled—have little or no function to play in today's urban labor market.

• The old homeless were primarily whites. In contrast, the new homeless are drawn heavily from minority groups. In cities with high proportions of blacks, the homeless are overwhelmingly black. In other cities with large Hispanic or American Indian minorities, these groups constitute major portions of the homeless.

The characteristics of the new homeless elicit more sympathy, perhaps, than the "old men drunk and sober" of the Skid Rows of the past. It is more arresting and disturbing to see homeless persons dotted all over the downtown urban landscape than to have them concentrated in readily avoidable areas of the city, and even more disturbing when some of the ragged and dirty are women and men in what are considered their prime years.

The new homeless serve as reminders that the social welfare safety nets begun during the Great Depression and significantly augmented in the 1960s are failing to prevent extreme destitution among an increasingly large portion of the American population. The failure of the welfare system to cover those who are vulnerable to homelessness is a long-standing fault of a system that essentially ignores the income-support problems faced by unattached adults. The Reagan administration has not succeeded in dismantling any significant portion of the net, but has made the mesh so coarse and weak that many fall through and hit bottom. Those who are disabled by the handicaps of minority status, chronic mental illness, physical illness, or substance abuse are especially vulnerable.

The social welfare system has never been very attentive to unattached men, but now it appears to be as unresponsive to unattached females. The slow erosion of the safety net has left gaps in the system through which have fallen the men and women of the streets, the shelters, and the welfare hotels. Likewise, the social welfare system does little to help families support their dependent adult members. Many of the old homeless, those of the 1950s and early 1960s, were pushed out or thrown away by their families when they passed the peak of adulthood, having reached age fifty or sixty. Many of the new homeless are products of a similar process, but one that begins at age twenty-five or thirty. With their disabilities, they have exhausted the patience and resources of relatives and friends no longer willing or able to support them.

As a result, homelessness now looms large on our political agenda, and there is much concern about what can be done. I have suggested a number of measures that might be taken to reduce homelessness to a more acceptable level. These include:

- compensating for the failures of our housing market by fostering the retention and enlargement of our urban low-income housing stock, especially housing appropriate for unattached persons;
- reversing the policy of the last two decades that has put personal choice above institutionalization for those so severely disabled that they are unable to make choices that will preserve their lives and physical well-being;
- enlarging the concept of disability to include conditions not purely physical in character, and in particular, recognizing chronic mental illness and chronic alcoholism for the profound disabilities that they are;
- restoring the real value of welfare payments to levels above bare subsistence, to the purchasing power of the late 1960s; and
- extending welfare benefits to unattached adults who are not senior citizens and the households that provide them with shelter and support.

There is considerable public support in the United States for a social welfare system that guarantees a minimally decent standard of living to all. Homelessness on the scale currently being experienced is clear evidence that such a system is not yet in place. That the current level of national prosperity is literally without historic parallel is likewise clear evidence that something can be done about the problem if the national will is there. I have tried to stress that public policy decisions have in large measure created the problem of homelessness. They can solve the problem as well.

Notes

Grateful acknowledgments are due to my valued colleague, Professor James D. Wright, now of Tulane University, who provided much of the information on the medical and public health aspects of homelessness and, in addition, gave me editorial advice and help throughout the writing of this manuscript.

Additional acknowledgments are due to the Robert Wood Johnson Foundation and the Pew Memorial Trust, which provided most of the funds for the Chicago homeless study. The Rockefeller Foundation has supported me generously throughout my sabbatical year.

I have been helped by many. I thank them all.

Chapter 1

1. See Stuart A. Rice, "The Homeless," *Annals of the American Academy of Political and Social Science* 77 (1918): 140–53; Nels Anderson, *The Hobo: The Sociology of the Homeless Man* (Chicago: University of Chicago Press, 1923; reissued as a Phoenix Edition, 1961). My working bibliography on the homeless now exceeds sixty single-spaced pages of entries, of which about three-quarters date from 1980 or later.

Chapter 2

1. For an overview of homelessness in America from the American Revolution until the Great Depression, see E. H. Monkkonen, ed., *Walking to Work: Tramps in America, 1790–1935* (Lincoln: University of Nebraska Press, 1984). And for an overview of the current homelessness problem in advanced industrial nations other than the United States, see Jurgen Friedrichs, *Affordable Housing and the Homeless* (Berlin: Walter de Gruyter, 1988). This volume includes chapters on Czechoslovakia, England, Sweden, West Germany, the Netherlands, France, and other countries. In the third world, homelessness has been an endemic problem for many decades.

2. See D. L. Jones, "The Strolling Poor: Transiency in Eighteenth Century Massachusetts," *Journal of Social History* 8 (1974): 28-54.

3. The settlement issue and the 1966 ruling are discussed in Joan M. Crouse, *The Homeless Transient in the Great Depression: New York State, 1929-1941* (Albany: SUNY Press, 1986).

4. Samuel Clemens, "The Facts Concerning the Recent Carnival of Crime in Connecticut," in *The Complete Humorous Sketches and Tales of Mark Twain*, ed. Charles Neider (Garden City, N.Y.: Doubleday & Co., 1985).

5. Charles Hoch, "A Brief History of the Homeless Problem in the United States," in *The Homeless in Contemporary Society*, ed. Richard D. Bingham, Roy E. Green, and Sammis B. White (Beverly Hills, Calif.: Sage Publications, 1987); Rick Beard, ed., *On Being Homeless: Historical Perspectives* (New York: Museum of the City of New York, 1987).

6. See Nels Anderson, *Men on the Move* (Chicago: University of Chicago Press, 1940), for a discussion of the institutionalization of Skid Row and its then-important labor market function.

7. See Crouse, *Homeless Transient*, 1986.

8. All figures are from Anderson, *Men on the Move*, 1940.

9. See Richard Freeman and Brian Hall, "Permanent Homelessness in America," paper prepared for the National Bureau of Economic Research, Cambridge, Mass., August 1986; Charles Marwick, "The 'Sizeable' Homeless Population: A Growing Challenge for Medicine," *Journal of the American Medical Association* 253, no. 22 (June 14, 1985): 3217-25.

10. The FERA legislation was unusual in recognizing that settlement issues left a large proportion of the poor in a limbo, setting up a transient program explicitly for persons who were not eligible for local and state relief. Some states, such as New York, set up transient centers that provided a few days of shelter and food, sending the transient on to some other jurisdiction thereafter. The federally supported transient camps in New York State were reserved primarily for "old" men, those forty and over, whose employment prospects were regarded as hopeless. What happened to the transient homeless when the FERA was succeeded by the WPA, a program that provided no specific coverage for that group, is unknown. (Elizabeth Wickendon, FERA administrator in the 1930s, recently published a rich memoir of that program in her chapter, "Reminiscences of the Program for Transients and Homeless in the Thirties," in Beard, *On Being Homeless*, 1987.)

11. K. Hopper and J. Hamburg, *The Making of America's Homeless: From Skid Row to New Poor, 1945-1984* (New York: Report prepared for the Institute of Social Welfare Research, Community Service Society, 1984).

12. See Howard Bahr and Theodore Caplow, *Old Men Drunk and Sober* (New York: NYU Press, 1974); Howard Bahr, *Disaffiliated Man* (Toronto: University of Toronto Press, 1970); Leonard Blumberg, Thomas Shipley, and Irving Shandler, *Skid Row and Its Alternatives* (Philadelphia: Temple University Press, 1973); Donald Bogue, *Skid Row in American Cities* (Chicago: Community and

Family Study Center, University of Chicago, 1963). Major studies also were undertaken in Minneapolis and Sacramento.

13. Bahr and Caplow's estimation of the number of homeless living outside the Bowery was based on an extrapolation from the recorded deaths of homeless persons living in non-Bowery areas of the city. There are serious problems with this estimate since it apparently assumed death rates for homeless persons that were unrealistically low. One study has found that the age-adjusted death rate for homeless men is about four times the average. See C. J. Alstrom, R. Lindelius, and I. Salum, "Mortality Among Homeless Men," *British Journal of Addictions* 70 (1975): 245–52; see also James Wright and Eleanor Weber, *Homelessness and Health* (New York: McGraw-Hill, 1987), chap. 8.

14. Bogue's count is about four hundred persons nightly in jails, in hospitals, and sleeping out on the streets. Since he later estimates about one hundred nightly sleeping on the streets, the remaining three hundred were apparently to be found in hospitals or in jails. Research on the Skid Rows before decriminalization of public drunkenness notes the police custom of cruising Skid Row areas arresting men sleeping on the streets or acting visibly intoxicated. An arrest resulted in at least one night spent in jail and possibly a sentence for a jail stay of a week or more, especially for repeat offenders.

15. All of the social scientists writing about Skid Row found nearly the same proportion of alcoholics, around a quarter. Yet all wrote as if the alcoholics were in the majority. This interpretive emphasis is manifested in Bahr and Caplow's title, *Old Men Drunk and Sober,* in one of Blumberg's titles, *Liquor and Poverty* (New Brunswick, N.J.: Rutgers Center of Alcohol Studies, 1978), and in Bogue's presentation of each descriptive statistic according to the drinking statuses of his respondents.

16. Barrett A. Lee, "The Disappearance of Skid Row: Some Ecological Evidence," *Urban Affairs Quarterly* 16, no. 1 (September 1980): 81–107.

17. On the disappearance of the SRO housing stock, see U.S. Congress, Senate Select Committee on Aging, *Single Room Occupancy: A Need for National Concern* (Washington, D.C.: Government Printing Office, 1978); Charles Hoch, *SROs: An Endangered Species* (Chicago: Community Emergency Shelter Organization and Jewish Council on Urban Affairs, December 1985). The select committee report refers to the loss of the SROs as "a nationwide trend."

18. Richard A. Easterlin, "The New Age Structure of Poverty in America," *Population and Development Review* 13, no. 2 (June 1987): 195–208.

19. SSI was authorized at the outset of the Social Security program and was designed to provide a very modest level of income to persons who were disabled or were over sixty-five and did not qualify for the old-age benefits. SSDI was authorized in 1963 and provided income benefits for persons who had accumulated credits under the Social Security system but had become disabled before reaching retirement age. SSI payments are very modest, averaging $164 per month in 1985, in contrast to the much more generous average SSDI payments of $484.

Chapter 3

1. D. L. Jones, "The Strolling Poor: Transiency in Eighteenth Century Massachusetts," *Journal of Social History* 8 (1974):28–54; Priscilla Clements, "The Transformation of the Wandering Poor in Nineteenth Century Philadelphia," in *Walking to Work: Tramps in America, 1790–1935,* ed. F. H. Monkkonen, (Lincoln: University of Nebraska Press, 1984). A useful overview of historical data on homeless women appears in Julie Lam, "Homeless Women in America: Their Social and Health Characteristics," Ph.D. diss., University of Massachusetts, Amherst, 1987.

2. Victor Bach and Renee Steinhagen, *Alternatives to the Welfare Hotel* (New York: Community Service Society, 1987); Elmer L. Struening, *A Study of Residents of the New York City Shelter System* (New York: Report of the N.Y. State Psychiatric Institute, 1986 and 1987).

3. Stephen Crystal and Merv Goldstein, *Chronic and Situational Dependency: Long Term Residents in a Shelter for Men* (New York: Human Resources Administration, 1982).

4. In addition, there were shelters specifically serving battered women or runaway youth, categories that overlap with the homeless. The full report of the Chicago homeless study can be found in Peter H. Rossi, Gene A. Fisher, and Georgianna Willis, *The Condition of the Homeless of Chicago* (Amherst, Mass.: Social and Demographic Research Institute, and Chicago: NORC—A Social Science Research Institute, 1986). A briefer description of the Chicago homeless study can be found in Peter H. Rossi, James D. Wright, Gene A. Fisher, and Georgianna Willis, "The Urban Homeless: Estimating Composition and Size," *Science* 235, no. 4794 (March 13, 1987): 1336–41. A much expanded account of that study and others undertaken on homelessness and extreme poverty will appear in a monograph by Rossi, *Down and Out in America,* to be published by the University of Chicago Press in 1989. Surveys of the homeless were taken in September 1985 and in February 1986. Each survey was composed of 1) a sample of persons housed in shelters, selected by sampling shelters for the homeless and then systematically interviewing a sample of shelter residents; and 2) a random sample of Chicago city blocks, with each sampled block systematically searched between midnight and 6 a.m., and all persons encountered being interviewed to determine their housing status. All persons found to be homeless were interviewed at length. The searches included abandoned buildings, lobbies, and hallways; parked cars or trucks; and any other unlocked place.

The Chicago homeless study was supported by generous grants from the Robert Wood Johnson Foundation, the Pew Memorial Trust, and the Illinois Department of Public Aid.

5. Bach and Steinhagen, *Alternatives to the Welfare Hotel,* 1987.

6. *U.S. Code Congressional and Administrative News,* P.L. 100–77, H.R. 558, July 22, 1987.

7. For example, estimates derived from the 1987 Current Population Survey were that in 1986 there were more than 7 million unmarried adults, ages twenty-

two to fifty-nine, whose annual incomes were under $4,000. Most of these extremely poor persons are living doubled up in conventional dwellings, many in households headed by their parents. These are persons who because of their low income are at high risk of becoming homeless, if and when their housemates decide that they can no longer provide shelter and other amenities.

8. U.S. Department of Housing and Urban Development, *A Report to the Secretary on the Homeless and Emergency Shelters* (Washington, D.C.: HUD, 1984).

9. Richard Freeman and Brian Hall, "Permanent Homelessness in America," paper prepared for the National Bureau of Economic Research, Cambridge, Mass., August 1986.

10. U.S. General Accounting Office, *Homelessness: A Complex Problem and the Federal Response* (Washington, D.C.: GAO, 1985).

11. See Rossi et al., "The Urban Homeless," 1987.

12. To illustrate the magnitude of the turnover, in the Chicago survey 31 percent had been homeless less than two months, whereas 25 percent had been homeless for two or more years.

13. See Irving Piliavin and Michael Sosin, "Tracking the Homeless," *Focus* 10, no. 4 (Winter 1987–88): 20–24.

14. When published, these estimates were the focus of considerable contention. Previous estimates, mostly advanced by advocates for the homeless, ranged upwards from fifteen thousand. In addition to the differences in the "methods" of estimation used—the previous high estimates were largely informed guesses—there also are differences in the time reference used and in what constitutes homelessness. Some of the advocates advance a definition of homeless that would include all persons inadequately housed, such as persons doubled up with other households, persons living in boarding houses or SROs, and persons living in overcrowded dwellings.

15. All of the studies define homelessness as I do: lacking conventional shelter and thus living in emergency shelters, in public places, or on the streets. A few of the studies also include people living in SROs or other marginal dwellings.

16. The full report on the study, known as the Ohio Study, is found in Dee Roth, Gerald Bean, Nancy Lust, and Traian Saveneau, *Homelessness in Ohio: A Study of People in Need* (Columbus: Ohio Department of Mental Health, Office of Program Evaluation, February 1985). Publications from the study include Dee Roth and Gerald Bean, "New Perspectives on Homelessness: Findings from a Statewide Epidemiological Study," *Hospital and Community Psychiatry* 37, no. 7 (July 1986): 712–19; Dee Roth, Gerald Bean, and Pamela S. Hyde, "Homelessness and Mental Health Policy: Developing an Appropriate Role for the 1980s," *Community Mental Health Journal* 22, no. 3 (Fall 1986): 203–14.

17. See, in order: Rodger Farr, Paul Koegel, and Audrey Burnham, *A Study of Homelessness and Mental Illness in the Skid Row Area of Los Angeles* (Los Angeles: Los Angeles County Department of Mental Health, 1986); *The 1986*

Los Angeles Skid Row Demographic Survey (Los Angeles: Hamilton, Rabinowitz & Alschuler, December 1986); New York State Department of Social Services, *Homelessness in New York State: A Report to the Governor and Legislature* (New York: NYSDSS, October 1984); "Enumeration of the Nashville Homeless Population," Nashville Coalition for the Homeless press release, December 1986; Donald Baumann, Charles Grigsby, Cheryl Beauvais, and D. Franklin Schultz, *The Austin Homeless* (Austin: Final Report to the Hogg Foundation for Mental Health, University of Texas at Austin, n.d.); Carl Brown, Steve Mac-Farlane, Rob Parardes, and Louisa Stark, *The Homeless of Phoenix: Who Are They and What Should Be Done?* (Phoenix: Report prepared for the Consortium for the Homeless by Phoenix South Community Mental Health Center, June 1983); Carol Mowbray et al., "Mental Health and Homelessness in Detroit: A Research Study," Michigan Department of Mental Health, 1983; Health and Welfare Council of Central Maryland, *Where Do You Go from Nowhere?* (Baltimore: Maryland Department of Human Resources, August 1986); Frederic Robinson, *Homeless People in the Nation's Capital* (Washington: University of the District of Columbia, Center for Applied Research and Urban Policy, November 1985).

18. Some of the women were apparently the live-in employees of the cubicle hotel managers; others were members of households living in conventional dwelling units that happened to be located in the Skid Row areas.

19. For reviews of these studies, see Patricia Sullivan and Shirley Damrosch, "Homeless Women and Children," in *The Homeless in Contemporary Society,* ed. Richard D. Bingham, Roy E. Green, and Sammis B. White (Beverly Hills, Calif.: Sage Publications, 1987), pp. 82–98; Marjorie Hope and James Young, *The Faces of Homelessness* (Lexington, Mass.: D. C. Heath, 1986); Lam, "Homeless Women in America," 1987.

20. James Wright and Eleanor Weber, *Homelessness and Health* (New York: McGraw-Hill, 1987).

21. James Wright et al., "Homelessness and Health," in *Research in Social Problems and Public Policy,* vol. 4, ed. Mike Lewis and Joanne Miller (Greenwich, Conn.: JAI Press, 1987), pp. 41–72. For more extended discussions of the apparent "deficit" of elderly among the homeless, see Wright and Weber, *Homelessness and Health,* 1987, chap. 4; and Peter H. Rossi and James D. Wright, "The Determinants of Homelessness," *Health Affairs* 6, no. 1 (Spring 1987): 19–32.

22. Wright et al., "Homelessness and Health," 1987.

23. Or so it appears. Blumberg speculates that black homeless men in Philadelphia in 1960 were underrepresented in his study because they were kept out of Skid Row by the discriminatory practices of cubicle hotel landlords, being absorbed instead into the black ghetto areas in rented rooms and boarding houses. Similar discriminatory practices might well have occurred in Chicago, New York, and elsewhere. If so, the effect would be to understate the proportion of blacks among the old homeless and to artificially heighten the contrast with the new homeless of today.

24. The average monthly room rent for Chicago SROs is $195, well more than the average monthly income for homeless persons in that city. See Charles Hoch, *SROs: An Endangered Species* (Chicago: Community Emergency Shelter Organization and Jewish Council on Urban Affairs, December 1985).

25. Wright and Weber, *Homelessness and Health,* 1987, chaps. 3 and 6. For a review of the controversies that surround the topic, see James Wright, "The Mentally Ill Homeless: What Is Myth and What Is Fact?" *Social Problems* 35, no. 2 (April 1988).

26. On the low end, with a figure of about 10 percent, are David Snow, Susan G. Baker, and Leon Anderson, "The Myth of Pervasive Mental Illness among the Homeless," *Social Problems* 33, no. 5 (June 1986); on the high end, with a figure of about 85 percent, is Ellen Bassuk, "The Homelessness Problem," *Scientific American* 251, no. 1 (July 1984): 40–45.

27. See, for example, Bassuk, "Homelessness Problem," 1984; Richard Lamb, "Deinstitutionalization and the Homeless Mentally Ill," *Hospital and Community Psychiatry* 35, no. 9 (1984): 899–907.

28. In 1958, the municipal court with jurisdiction over Chicago's Skid Row had a staff psychiatrist whose function was to recommend commitment to mental hospitals for Skid Row residents brought before the court and judged to be psychotic. Bogue suggests that this screening process lowered the incidence of psychosis among the Skid Row residents he studied. An even earlier study of emergency municipal shelters by Edwin H. Sutherland and Harvey J. Locke, *Twenty Thousand Homeless Men* (Chicago: University of Chicago Press, 1936), describes a similar process that shunted clearly psychotic men to the mental hospitals (and thus out of the emergency shelters). In contrast, current shelter practices in Chicago and elsewhere often debar persons behaving in a bizarre, florid, or obviously psychotic manner. Rather than being shunted off to mental hospitals, the clearly psychotic are now left to sleep on the streets.

29. Wright and Weber, *Homelessness and Health,* 1987, p. 56. The detailed account of health findings appears in chapter 7. See also P. W. Brickner et al., *Health Care of Homeless People* (New York: Springer, 1985); Marjorie Robertson and Michael R. Cousineau, "Health Status and Access to Health Services among the Urban Homeless," *American Journal of Public Health* 76, no. 5 (May 1986): 561–63. These studies report the health status of homeless persons who have sought medical care through clinics set up for homeless persons. Hence they tend to overestimate the incidence and prevalence of medical conditions. However, comparisons with the conditions reported by the domiciled population seeking medical care from conventional sources show that the incidence and prevalence of all conditions among the homeless are magnitudes above those reported by the domiciled.

30. See Virginia Mulken and R. Spence, *Alcohol Abuse/Alcoholism among the Homeless: A Review of the Literature* (Washington, D.C.: National Institute on Alcohol Abuse and Alcoholism, November 1984).

31. Wright and Weber, *Homelessness and Health,* 1987, chap. 5.

32. A summary of the literature on male-female differences in drinking

behavior among the homeless is found in Janet Knight, "Alcohol Abuse among the Homeless," Ph.D. diss., University of Massachusetts, Amherst, 1987.

33. See *Alcohol, Drug Abuse, and Mental Health Problems of the Homeless: Proceedings of a Roundtable* (Washington, D.C.: Department of Health and Human Services, Public Health Service, 1983); Wright and Weber, *Homelessness and Health*, 1987, chap. 5.

34. In many housing markets, a prospective renter must put down a month's rent in advance plus a security deposit. Thus, an apartment renting for $400 per month might require as much as $800 cash even to make an offer. Adding some funds for furnishings, the move-in cost might well exceed $1,000. There is impressionistic evidence to suggest that at least some shelter dwellers have full-time and relatively well paying jobs and use free shelter accommodations to help them accumulate the cash necessary to enter the conventional rental market.

35. In fact, nearly a third of the poor in this country spend 70 percent or more of their incomes on housing alone. See U.S. General Accounting Office, *Homelessness: A Complex Problem*, 1985, p. 25.

36. The idea of comparing the homeless to equally poor but domiciled persons is itself not a new one. Bahr and Caplow interviewed in a poor, predominantly white Brooklyn neighborhood to obtain a comparison group. Since most of the men living in that neighborhood were boarders in rooming houses, they qualified as domiciled but extremely poor.

37. The full study is reported in Matthew Stagner and Harold Richman, *General Assistance Profiles: Findings from a Longitudinal Study of Newly Approved Recipients* (Chicago: Illinois Department of Public Aid, June 1985). The study is a panel survey: 400 new GA recipients were interviewed in March 1984, and 335 of them were reinterviewed in August.

38. To be sure, many of the Chicago homeless are also eligible for categorical programs such as SSI and SSDI because of their disabilities. Phrased properly, my point is that most homeless people in Illinois who are not eligible for categorical support under one or another program are eligible for General Assistance.

Chapter 4

1. All these figures are taken from James Wright and Julie Lam, "Homelessness and the Low Income Housing Supply," *Social Policy* 17, no. 4 (Spring 1987): 22–27.

2. During the same period, incidentally, 11,000 subsidized senior citizen units were added to the stock and 8,500 Section 8 senior citizen housing vouchers were issued. Thus, provision was made for the replacement of lost housing stock, but, overwhelmingly, the replacements consisted of subsidized housing for persons age sixty-five and over. See "Housing Needs of Chicago's Single, Low Income Renters," Chicago Department of Planning, draft report, June 1985; and Charles Hoch, *SROs: An Endangered Species* (Chicago: Community Emergency Shelter Operation and Jewish Council on Urban Affairs, December

1985). This latter reports that 22,603 SRO rooms in Chicago were lost (condemned, demolished, or converted to other uses) between 1973 and 1985.

3. See Wright and Lam, "Homelessness and the Low Income Housing Supply," 1987, for specific data and figures.

4. *The 1986 Los Angeles Skid Row Demographic Survey* (Los Angeles: Hamilton, Rabinowitz & Alschuler, December 1986).

5. Hoch, *SROs: An Endangered Species,* 1985.

6. Wright and Lam, "Homelessness and the Low Income Housing Supply," 1987.

7. Hoch, *SROs: An Endangered Species,* 1985.

8. Indeed, the interchange is such that many people include SRO tenants within their definition of homelessness, a perfectly justifiable strategy on many grounds.

9. "Overspending" on housing is not meant to imply profligacy or personal financial mismanagement. In my definition, a person overspends on housing if the monthly housing cost leaves too little income to pay for the rest of life's necessities. Poor people overspend on housing not by paying more than they should but by paying more than they can in reality afford.

10. Rodger Farr, Paul Koegel, and Audrey Burnham, *A Study of Homelessness and Mental Illness in the Skid Row Area of Los Angeles* (Los Angeles: Los Angeles County Department of Mental Health, 1986).

11. William Tucker, "Where Do the Homeless Come From?" *National Review,* September 25, 1987, pp. 32-43.

12. As indicated earlier, the HUD estimates are simple averages of informed guesses about the number of homeless people in each city. The figures have received a great deal of criticism, and no one can gauge their accuracy. Still, it is likely that the relative magnitude of the homelessness problem city-to-city is accurately reflected in HUD's figures. In other words, the figures probably rank-order cities correctly in terms of their relative homelessness problems, even if they say little about the absolute magnitudes. An accurate rank ordering is all that is necessary for Tucker's analysis.

13. Barrett A. Lee, "The Disappearance of Skid Row: Some Ecological Evidence," *Urban Affairs Quarterly* 16, no. 1 (September 1980):81-107.

14. Richard A. Easterlin, "The New Age Structure of Poverty in America," *Population and Development Review* 13, no. 2 (June 1987): 195-208.

15. See James Wright, "The Worthy and Unworthy Homeless," *Society* (forthcoming).

16. Although only a few of the homeless men in the Chicago survey had ever married, and most who had married were subsequently divorced or separated, a sizable majority (60 percent) claimed to have fathered children. One wonders how many of the fathers of children in homeless female-headed households are themselves homeless men.

Chapter 5
1. Alice S. Rossi and Peter H. Rossi, *Of Human Bonding* (Hawthorne, N.Y.: Aldine DeGruyter, forthcoming).

2. Or, in the not infrequent case, has no kin or friendship network to offer maintenance and support in the first place.

3. Irving Piliavin and Michael Sosin, "Tracking the Homeless," *Focus* 10, no. 4 (Winter 1987–88): 20–24.

4. To be sure, the period did witness some "compensations." By the end of the period covered in this analysis, the Food Stamp program had become a major benefit available to the very poor, and in 1985, a participant in the program would have had an additional seventy dollars to spend on food in a month. Much of what can be bought with food stamps, however, requires food preparation facilities, and so food stamps are of limited value to the homeless. Medicaid coverage was also extended in some states (Illinois among them), but one cannot pay the rent or buy food with Medicaid coverage.

5. "State Says It Can't Afford to Comply with Welfare Ruling," *Daily Hampshire Gazette* (Northampton, Mass.), January 6, 1987, p. 14. The court ruled, incidentally, that in order for a family to avoid homelessness and live a minimally decent existence, the AFDC payment levels would have to be approximately doubled. This would be exactly what is necessary to restore the purchasing power of AFDC to its 1968 value (see Table 5.1).

6. The very low GA payment levels may explain why so few of the homeless in Chicago ever applied for or received GA assistance, despite their eligibility. As I have already stressed, the average cost of the cheapest housing available in Chicago exceeds the GA payment by about $50.

A further barrier is the burdensome application process. As described by Matthew Stagner and Harold Richman, *General Assistance Profiles: Findings from a Longitudinal Study of Newly Approved Recipients* (Chicago: Illinois Department of Public Aid, June 1985), applying for GA assistance involved at least three interviews with Illinois Department of Public Aid case workers, an employability determination, and an assignment either to an unemployable class or to a "jobs" program in which a person had to sustain eligibility by applying for jobs to at least eight employers a month. If a person assigned to the "jobs" program did not get a job within sixty days, he was either reassigned to the unemployable class or to a public service "workfare" task. All this for $154 a month.

7. In 1984, the total federal social welfare expenditure was $419 billion. Social Security pensions and Medicare expenditures alone amounted to $302 billion, 72 percent of the total social welfare expenditure. See *Statistical Abstract of the United States, 1985* (Washington, D.C.: Department of Commerce), Table 574.

Chapter 6

1. Of course, these are uncompleted episodes of homelessness: some of those who are currently homeless for less than six months could remain in that condition and join those who are homeless for long periods of time. As a rule of thumb, one can expect that durations measured at some point of time would double if one could follow the individuals to the end point of their episode.

Hence a likely proportion of the homeless whose episodes end within six months is between 25 percent and 30 percent.

2. The best current estimates are that no more than about half of the homeless receive any form of entitlement or social benefit, with the rate of participation in any specific program being less than 25 percent, this despite the obviously high level of need characteristic of this group. See Peter H. Rossi, Gene A. Fisher, and Georgianna Willis, *The Condition of the Homeless of Chicago* (Amherst, Mass.: Social and Demographic Research Institute, and Chicago: NORC—A Social Science Research Institute, 1986); James Wright and Eleanor Weber, *Homelessness and Health* (New York: McGraw-Hill, 1987), chap. 9. The General Accounting Office report, *Homelessness: A Complex Problem and the Federal Response* (Washington, D.C.: GAO, 1985), provides a very useful discussion of the barriers that homeless people face in attempting to exploit the welfare system.

3. For those unfamiliar with the labyrinth of programs that define the social welfare system, Social Security Disability Insurance (SSDI) provides monthly income transfer payments to disabled persons who have a work history. Supplemental Security Income (SSI) provides payments for disabled persons who do not have work histories. In Illinois and most other states, General Assistance is for persons not otherwise eligible for transfer programs; AFDC supports parents, typically single mothers, with dependent children in their care. SSDI is by far the most generous program (averaged across the nation), followed by AFDC, then SSI, and then General Assistance (see Table 5.1).

4. A recent study of patients in Chicago-area mental hospitals conducted by Dan A. Lewis, Tom Pavkov, Helen Rosenberg, Susan Reed, Arthur Lurigio, Zev Kalifon, Bruch Johnson, and Stephanie Riger, *State Hospitalization Utilization in Chicago* (Evanston, Ill.: Center for Urban Affairs and Policy Research, Northwestern University, 1987), found that over 95 percent had been voluntarily committed, most after being brought before the courts on complaints signed by their kin or by the police. A person committed voluntarily can request release after only five days in the hospital, a request that cannot be denied. The consequence is that the state hospitals in Cook County serve as short-term residences for most of their patients, a revolving-door situation that brings the chronically mentally ill into the hospitals several times during a year: over a year's time about twenty thousand patients pass through a system that has about two thousand beds.

5. Almost all of the shelter managers in Chicago followed policies that would refuse admission to persons acting in a bizarre manner, or obviously drunk or under the influence of drugs, or who had "caused trouble" in the past. Although these policies are followed in order to safeguard the peace and rest of the shelter residents, they also have the unfortunate consequence of leaving the most disabled of the homeless out on the streets.

6. See the review of manpower evaluation studies in Peter H. Rossi, Richard A. Berk, and Kenneth J. Lenihan, *Money, Word and Crime* (New York: Academic Press, 1983).

7. Board of Directors, Manpower Demonstration Research Corporation, *Summary of Findings of the National Supported Work Demonstration* (Cambridge, Mass.: Ballinger Publishing Co., 1986).

8. Of course, these anticipated demographic changes will improve the prospects mainly for persons who are now in their teens and will be young adults in the near future. Whether they will do much for the currently demoralized young as they move into their middle years is yet to be determined.

9. *The 1986 Los Angeles Skid Row Demographic Survey* (Los Angeles: Hamilton, Rabinowitz & Alschuler, December 1986).

10. Ironically, in many cities the "Ys," reluctant to serve as the "housing of last resort" for the mentally ill and nearly destitute aged, are phasing out their hotels.

11. However, so is the provision of emergency housing. The costs of maintaining homeless families in so-called welfare hotels far exceed the cost of paying rent for such families in conventional rental housing. Jonathan Kozol in his recent book *Rachel and Her Children* (New York: Crown Publishers, 1988) cites costs of about twenty thousand dollars per year per family for the rental of rooms in the Hotel Martinique in Manhattan for homeless families.

12. H. Richard Lamb, ed., *The Homeless Mentally Ill* (Washington, D.C.: American Psychiatric Association, 1984).

13. The survey was conducted in 1985, using an innovative measurement strategy in which succinct vignettes depicting single-parent families, their composition, age, and other characteristics were systematically varied. Respondents were asked how large should weekly payments be to those persons (unpublished data).

14. The Current Population Survey counts only parents, children, and siblings as relatives. More distant kin, such as grandparents, aunts, or uncles, are classified as nonrelatives. Many of these unattached adults classified as living with nonrelatives may in fact have been living with kin.

Index

AFDC. *See* Aid to Families with Dependent Children
Age: and employment, 35, 39, 51-54; of homeless, 10, 20, 57, 62-63
Aged, 20, 55, 56; housing for, 12, 42-43, 54, 72n2
Aid to Families with Dependent Adults (proposed), 57-59
Aid to Families with Dependent Children (AFDC), 16, 27, 40, 52, 55, 57, 58; and homeless, 26, 42, 47, 48
Alcoholics, 1, 2, 8, 23
Alcoholism, 10, 11, 23, 25, 28, 46n, 55-56
American Indians, 20-21, 62
Anderson, Nels, 3, 7, 8
Arrest of homeless, 9-10, 13-14, 28, 46n, 55

Bahr, Howard, 8, 9, 10, 11, 19, 23, 26
Behavior of homeless, 13, 15, 49
Blacks, 20, 28, 36, 40, 62, 70n23
Blumberg, Leonard, 8, 9, 19, 22
Bogue, Donald, 8-9, 10, 11-12, 15, 19, 22, 23, 32, 71n28
Boston (Mass.), 37, 42
Bowery (New York City), 8-9, 10, 19, 20

California, 21, 31, 32, 34, 54
Caplow, Theodore, 8, 9, 10, 11, 19, 23, 26
Carter, Jimmy, 52
Casual labor. *See* Unskilled labor
Census Bureau, 9, 27, 31, 40
Charities, 15, 16, 21
Chicago (Ill.), 8-9, 10, 11-12, 20, 21, 25, 34, 71n28; assistance in, 27-29, 38-39, 47, 48; homeless population of, 9, 19, 36; housing in, 15, 17, 18, 32-34, 51
Children, 15, 39, 61
Chronically homeless, 25, 45-46
Chronically mentally ill. *See* Mentally ill
Civil rights, 49
Clements, Priscilla, 14
Commitment of mentally ill, 49-50, 71n28
Committee on the Care of Transient and Homeless, 7
Comprehesive Employment and Training Act (CETA), 52
Cost of programs, 53, 56, 57, 58
Courts, 6, 14, 42, 71n28

Deaths of homeless, 1-2
Deinstitutionalization of mentally ill, 22, 23, 49
Department of Housing and Urban Development (HUD), 8, 17, 31
Disabilities, 10, 22, 25, 28, 39, 51, 55, 62; definition of, 46n, 55-56, 63. *See also* specific disabilities, e.g., Physical disability
Disaffiliated Man (Bahr), 10
Drug abuse, 25, 55
Drunkenness, public, 8-9, 13, 55. *See also* Alcoholism

Easterlin, Richard A., 35
Employment, 8, 10, 20, 28, 34-36, 39, 46, 51-54. *See also* Unemployed
Episodically homeless. *See* Temporary homeless
Ethnicity of homeless, 1, 10, 20-21. *See also* Minorities

Families, 36, 37-38, 58, 59; homeless, 8, 14, 15-16, 26, 36; of homeless, 1, 10, 11, 26, 33, 39, 46n, 62-63; of mentally ill, 50
Federal Emergency Relief Administration, 7
Financial assistance, 37-38, 40-42. *See also* Welfare programs
Food Stamps, 16, 48-49
Foster home placement, 39
Freeman, Richard, 17
Frost, Robert, 5

General Assistance (GA), 27-29, 33, 38-39, 40, 42, 47, 48, 58
Gentrification, 12
Government responsibility for homeless, 3, 16, 31, 56-57. *See also* Welfare programs
Grapes of Wrath, The (Steinbeck), 8
Great Depression, 6-8, 53, 62
"Greyhound therapy," 7

Hall, Brian, 17
Health-Care-for-the-Homeless (HCH), 16, 19-20, 23, 25
Health of the homeless, 23, 25, 34. *See also* Mentally ill; Physical disability
Hispanics, 20-21, 36, 62
Hobo, The (Anderson), 3

Home, 5, 9, 46
Homeless, 4, 6; definition of, 9, 16
Housing, 11-12, 16, 17-18. *See also* Shelters; Single-room-occupancy (SRO) hotels
Housing Act, 49
Housing costs, 21, 27, 31-34, 42-43, 47, 72nn34, 35. *See also* Subsidized housing
Housing market, 21, 32, 34, 46, 54, 61, 63
HUD. *See* Department of Housing and Urban Development

Illinois, 27-29, 40-42, 47, 50. *See also* Chicago (Ill.); General Assistance
Income, 42, 52; and age, 35-36; of homeless, 10, 20, 21, 27, 48, 61; and housing, 32-33, 56-57; of poor, 26-28, 41. *See also* Social Security
Inflation, 40, 56, 57
Institutionalization, 49

Jewish Council on Urban Affairs, 33
Jones, D. L., 14

Kinship. *See* Families

Labor market, 34-36, 46, 52-53
Lam, Julie, 32
Lee, Barrett, 11, 35
Legislation, 3, 16, 55
Local homeless, 6
Long-term homeless. *See* Chronically homeless
Los Angeles (Calif.), 21, 32, 34, 54

Manpower Demonstration Research Corporation (MDRC), 52
Massachusetts, 14, 37, 42
McKinney Act, 16
Media and the homeless, 3
Men on the Move (Anderson), 7
Men's Shelter (New York City), 20
Mentally ill, 10, 12, 15, 22-23, 25, 28, 49-50, 55
Migrant labor, 6, 25
Minneapolis (Minn.), 17, 23, 39
Minorities, 20-21, 40, 51-54, 57, 62. *See also* Blacks; Hispanics

National Coalition for the Homeless, 16-17
National Institute of Mental Health, 18
New homeless, 13-14; contrasts with old homeless, 19-21, 61, 62-63; similarities with old homeless, 21-26
New York City, 8, 10, 14, 20; homeless population in, 9, 19, 36; housing in, 15-16, 57

Noninstitutionalization of mentally ill, 22, 23, 49
Old homeless, 19-26, 61, 62
Old Men Drunk and Sober (Bahr and Caplow), 8

Pew Memorial Trust, 16, 19, 23
Philadelphia (Penn.), 8, 22, 23, 34; homeless population in, 9, 14, 19
Physical disability, 10, 12, 23, 25
Piliavin, Irving, 39
Police and homeless, 6, 7, 9, 13-14
Poor, 25-26, 31-32, 38-39, 57; contrast with homeless, 26-29
Population: of homeless, 7, 11, 16-18, 19-20, 34, 56; of poor, 26, 27, 43, 45, 58, 62
Poverty, 10, 20, 21, 36, 43, 45, 56
Public employment, 52-53
Public opinion, 5, 6, 7-8, 57
Public spending, 43. *See also* Social Security; Welfare programs

Reagan administration, 62
Religious missions, 15
Richman, Harold, 27
Robert Wood Johnson Foundation, 16, 19, 23
Rossi, Alice, 37
Rossi, Peter, 15, 18, 37
Rural homeless, 18

Settlement rights, 5-6
Shelter, 13, 19, 21, 32, 46, 61. *See also* Housing Shelters, 7, 8-10, 14-15, 17, 26, 32, 33, 50-51, 54-55
Short-term homeless. *See* Temporary homeless
Single-parent households, 14, 26, 36, 38, 42, 61
Single-room-occupancy (SRO), hotels, 9, 11, 12, 32-34, 42, 47, 49, 51, 54
Skid Row, 6, 7, 8-12, 14, 19, 20, 25, 62
Skid Row in American Cities (Bogue), 8-9
Social disaffiliation, 10-11, 26
Social Security, 10, 12, 20, 40, 42-43, 67n19
Social Security Disability Income (SSDI), 16, 47, 67n19
Social welfare programs. *See* Welfare programs
Sosin, Michael, 39
SRO hotels. *See* Single-room-occupancy (SRO) hotels
SSDI. *See* Social Security Disability Income
SSI. *See* Supplemental Security Income
Stagner, Matthew, 27
Standard of living, 21, 34, 42
Steinbeck, John, 8
Subsidized housing, 11, 12, 31, 43, 49, 51, 54

Substance abuse, 25, 55. *See also* Alcoholism
Supplemental Security Income (SSI), 12, 47, 67n19
Supported Work Experiment, 52
Supreme Court, 6

Technological changes: and employment, 6, 11, 35
Temporary employment, 2, 10, 20, 34, 47, 62
Temporary homeless, 25-26, 45, 58
Training: in job skills, 51-53
Transients, 6. *See also* Homeless
Tucker, William, 34
Twain, Mark, 6

Unattached persons, 32, 40, 46, 61, 62; assistance for, 28, 57, 58-59; definition of, 6; housing for, 32, 54-55, 63
Unemployed, 1, 7, 8, 38, 52, 57

Unskilled labor, 1, 6, 8, 11, 34-36, 46, 62

Veterans, 8

Weber, Eleanor, 20, 22, 23
Welfare departments, 7, 14, 16, 48, 57
Welfare hotels, 15-16, 36, 57
Welfare programs, 5-6, 16, 26-28, 40, 47-49, 53, 55, 62, 63. *See also* specific programs, e.g., Aid to Families with Dependent Children
Women: employment of, 7, 35-36
Women homeless, 1, 7, 36, 38, 39, 61; assistance for, 42, 62; health of, 25; housing for, 15, 17, 26; population of, 14, 19-20
World War II, 8
Wright, James, 20, 22, 23, 32, 49

Young adults, 40-42, 61; employment of, 51-54